ON POINT

READING AND CRITICAL THINKING SKILLS

3

Compass Publishing

Peggy Anderson • Jacob Cullen • Rob Jordens

ON POINT 3

READING AND CRITICAL THINKING SKILLS

Peggy Anderson • Jacob Cullen • Rob Jordens

© 2015 Compass Publishing

Editorial Director: Kate Kim
Series Editor: Jon Edwards
Project Coordinator: Stella Park
Content Editor: David Charlton
Copy Editor: Lee Ming Ang
Designer: Ji Sook Lee

email: info@compasspub.com
http://www.compasspub.com

ISBN: 978-1-61352-738-2

11 10 9 8 7 6 5 4 3
19 18 17 16

Photo Credits

All photos and images © Shutterstock, Inc.

Printed in Korea

The publisher would like to thank the following for granting permission to reproduce copyrighted material: p. 4, "Caring What Other People Think" by Fredric Neuman, M.D. © 2013, the author. Used by permission; p. 18, "I Took My Kids Offline" by Melissa McClements. © 2011, Guardian News & Media Ltd. Used by permission; p.32, "Sick of the Fame Game" by Paul Harris. © 2006, Guardian News & Media Ltd. Used by permission; p. 46, "Behaviorism and the Cognitive Model" by Ron Hammond, Ph.D., and Paul Cheney, Ph.D. © 2009, Paul Cheney. Used by permission; p. 52, "Is Strict Parenting Better for Children?" by Emine Saner. © 2011, Guardian News & Media Ltd. Used by permission; p. 60, "The Ordinary Lies We All Tell, and What's Behind Them" by Susan Krauss Whitbourne, Ph.D. © 2013, the author. Used by permission; p. 74, "Why We Want to Spend the Rest of Our Lives on Mars" by Josh Davis. © 2014, Guardian News & Media Ltd. Used by permission; p. 88, "They Don't Live for Work . . . They Work to Live" by Anushka Asthana. © 2008, Guardian News & Media Ltd. Used by permission; p. 122, "Do Weird People Make Better Artists?" by Ivan Hewett. © 2014, Telegraph Media Group Ltd. Used by permission; p. 130, "Do You Have Too Many Friends?" by Richard Koch. © 2013, the author. Used by permission; p. 144, "Should We Experiment on Animals? Yes" by Colin Blakemore. © 2008, Telegraph Media Group Ltd. Used by permission; p. 164, "Living on the 100-Mile Diet" by Alisa Smith and J. B. MacKinnon. © 2005, the authors. Used by permission.

ON POINT 3

READING AND CRITICAL THINKING SKILLS

Peggy Anderson • Jacob Cullen • Rob Jordens

Compass Publishing

CONTENTS

SCOPE AND SEQUENCE

UNIT	READING	VOCABULARY
Unit **1** **Technology** **Early Adopters: Leaders or Fools?**	**Reading 1**: Early Adopters Fall into a Costly Trap	arbitrary, consumer, device, neutral, presumably, revenue, shift, underestimate
	Reading 2: The Fun—and the Power—of Being an Early Adopter	consult, expertise, implicitly, motive, occupation, passively, undertaking, voluntary
Unit **2** **Education** **Focus on Learning**	**Reading 1**: Finland's Schools Flourish in Freedom and Flexibility	assemble, attributable, commence, comprehensive, contemporary, immigrant, interpret, subsidize
	Reading 2: Aiming High: Education and Economic Growth in Singapore	administrator, civil, commitment, credit, evaluation, mechanism, ongoing, professional
Unit **3** **Careers** **The Evolving Workplace**	**Reading 1**: Breaking Free of 9 to 5	convention, energetic, eventual, incapable, institute, justify, legislate, unmotivated
	Reading 2: How Companies Can Keep Their Talent	adapt, corporation, domain, implication, insightful, phenomenal, potentially, precedence
Unit **4** **Engineering** **The Future Is Now**	**Reading 1**: Nanotechnology World: Nanomedicine Offers New Cures	adjacent, analysis, assign, coordinator, distinction, ethics, regulation, resolve
	Reading 2: Drive My Car . . . Please	acknowledge, administration, anticipate, concurrently, consequently, equation, paradigm, preliminary
Unit **5** **Crime** **Tricks, Schemes, and Scams**	**Reading 1**: Return of the Con Artist: Tips to Protect Yourself	exploitation, indication, insecurity, liberally, manipulative, objectivity, target, unprincipled
	Reading 2: Scammers Choose Their Victims Wisely	constraint, currency, depressed, evaluate, extract, investment, participant, scheme
Unit **6** **Psychology** **Mastering the Mind**	**Reading 1**: How to Maximize Your Memory	analogous, context, conversely, correspondence, denote, imagery, retention, so-called
	Reading 2: Everyday Tips for a Better Memory	channel, decline, document, endorse, induce, journal, enhancement, retain

READING SKILL	CRITICAL THINKING SKILL	UNIT OUTCOME	WRITING ASSIGNMENT
Previewing and Predicting	Detecting Arguments (Premises and Conclusions)	Express your opinion about being an early adopter of technology	Do you think it is a good idea to be an early adopter of technology?
Analyzing the Author's Point of View	Recognizing Common Fallacies: Appeal to Authority	Discuss the ideal conditions for student learning	Based on the readings, what do you think are ideal conditions for students to learn in?
Asking Questions While Reading	Identifying Deductive and Inductive Arguments	Express your opinion about how companies can make conditions better for employees	What should today's employers do to make sure their employees are productive and happy?
Comparing and Contrasting	Identifying Circular Reasoning	Express your opinion about what technology will impact humans the most	In your opinion, what new invention or technology will have the greatest impact on human beings?
Recalling and Extracting Information	Distinguishing Generalization from Overgeneralization	Express your opinion about how to avoid scams	What can people do to avoid being victims of con artists?
Making Inferences	Understanding Research Studies	Explain how to improve your memory	Do you think you have a good memory? How do you think you could improve it?

READING SKILL	CRITICAL THINKING SKILL	UNIT OUTCOME	WRITING ASSIGNMENT
Identifying Causes and Effects	Identifying Causation and Correlation	Express your ideas about what is necessary to become great at something	What does one need to do in order to become an expert at something?
Determining Importance	Recognizing Common Fallacies: Arguments from Ignorance	Express your opinion about being an optimist or a pessimist	In your opinion, is it better to be an optimist or a pessimist?
Monitoring and Clarifying Understanding	Classifying Claims	Express your opinion about adults living with their parents	Do you think it's a good idea for young adults to live with their parents?
Summarizing	Recognizing Common Fallacies: Appeals to Popularity or Tradition	Express your opinion about the differences between male and female friendships	What are the main differences between male and female friendships?
Facts and Opinions	Recognizing Common Fallacies: *Ad Hominem*, Straw Man, Slippery Slope	Express your opinion about organizations collecting people's private information	Is it OK for companies and other organizations to collect information about people?
Determining the Author's Purpose	Evaluating Arguments	Describe changes that you would like to see in your city	What are some changes you'd like to see made to your city?

STUDENT BOOK

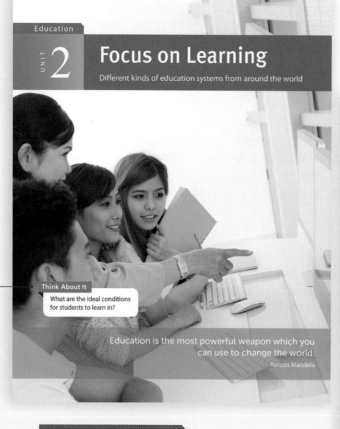

Education

UNIT 2

Focus on Learning

Different kinds of education systems from around the world

Think About It

What are the ideal conditions for students to learn in?

Education is the most powerful weapon which you can use to change the world.
Nelson Mandela

LEARNING GOALS

A clear outline of the learning objectives helps students to keep the big picture in mind as they progress.

What you'll learn in this unit:

Reading 1 / Finland's Schools Flourish in Freedom and Flexibility
Reading Skill: Analyzing the Author's Point of View

Reading 2 / Aiming High: Education and Economic Growth in Singapore
Critical Thinking Skill: Recognizing Common Fallacies: Appeal to Authority

Unit Project | **Make Your Point**
Discuss the ideal conditions for student learning

Before You Read

1. Look at the following aspects of school learning environments and add another of your own. Then rank them from 1 (most important) to 6 (least important). Compare and discuss your rankings with a partner.

_____ Qualified teachers	_____ Tutoring help for assignments and tests
_____ Technology in the classroom	_____ Useful facilities such as a library and a gym
_____ Interesting textbooks	_____ _____ (your idea)

2. Answer the questions. Discuss your answers with a partner.

1 What type of schoolwork do you like most? What do you like least?
   a. Group projects
   b. Written essays
   c. Presentations
   d. Tests
   e. Other (specify)

2 Is there anything you would change about your school if you could? Why?

16

FOCUS QUESTION

A thought-provoking question serves as the focus for the unit. As they read the passages and complete the discussion activities, students form their own response to the question.

LEAD-IN ACTIVITIES

Pre-reading exercises activate prior knowledge and relate the topic to students' own lives.

Paraphrased sentences from the reading passage present a preview of key academic target words in context. Activities get students to practice using context clues to determine the meaning of key words before encountering them in the passage.

REAL-LIFE READINGS

Reading passages from online magazines, blogs, newspapers, and textbooks explore a wide range of engaging, relevant topics.

Reading 1

VOCABULARY PREVIEW

Read the sentence. Circle the choice that is closest to the meaning of the AWL word in bold.

1 Teachers are allowed to **interpret** the subject they are teaching in their own way.
  a. avoid   b. forget   c. explain

2 Children **commence** primary school studies when they turn 7 years old.
  a. pass   b. start   c. allow

3 Most Finnish children attend **comprehensive** schools, which serve every kind of student, rather than the more selective private schools.
  a. all-inclusive   b. difficult   c. high-quality

4 Finland's success is **attributable to** the importance that is given to teaching.
  a. caused by   b. blamed on   c. improved by

5 The **contemporary** building makes the school look like a new university.
  a. large   b. modern   c. expensive

6 These alternative schools do not charge fees and are **subsidized** by the government.
  a. taxed   b. managed   c. given money

7 You can see students **assemble** around computers to pick their next classes.
  a. work   b. fighting   c. gather

8 That school is known to have a high number of **immigrant** children.
  a. talented   b. newcomer from abroad   c. happy

READING PREVIEW

This passage is an article about schools in Finland. The author discusses what is special about the Finnish education system.

Schools are under a lot of pressure to provide a quality education. How do people judge a school's level of success? What positive outcomes must schools show? Think of a few ways that schools are evaluated and share them with a partner.

17

Read the article.

Finland's Schools Flourish in Freedom and Flexibility

by Jeevan Vasagar
© 2013, Telegraph Media Group Limited. Used by permission.

At Meri-Rastila primary school in a suburb[1] of Helsinki, pupils shake the snow off their boots in the corridors[2], then peel them off and shuffle softly into class in socks. After a 45-minute lesson, they are out in the playground again.

The Finnish school day is short and intermixed with bursts of running around, shrieking[3], and sledding outdoors. Children **commence** their studies when they are older, the year they turn 7, and there is no pressure on them to do anything academic before then.

The Finnish education system contrasts sharply with that of England. Every Finnish child gets a free school meal and a free education, which extends to the university level.

Q. What is the main idea of the article? Underline it.

Finland is a country of 5.4 million people, with about 600,000 students from primary to secondary school.

There are no league tables, no school inspections, and only one set of national exams, which children take at age 18 when they are about to leave school. The government only conducts the national assessments to sample the population as a means of keeping track of school performance, but these results are not made public.

Meri-Rastila's principal, Ritva Tyyska, said, "I think it's quite good that they don't rank the schools because we have good teachers, we have a curriculum[4], and we have to obey it. In every school, we teach about the same things. The methods can be a little bit different, [but you] get the same education.

"We have these tests in the fifth or sixth form[5] that are the same tests at each and every school. We get the results, and we see where we stand. But that is not common knowledge. And if it's not good, we have to check what we are doing wrong, what we have to improve."

In Finland, the state decides what should be taught, but not how. If they like, teachers can take their children outside for "wood mathematics," where they go into the nearest patch of forest and learn to add and subtract by counting twigs or stones in the open air.

A typical lesson compresses[6] several disciplines into one. In a combined class, children who don't speak Finnish as their first language are taught to identify and name the parts of a mouse and then mark on a chalk outline of the country where the animal lives. It is a literacy lesson, but a biology and geography one as well.

Meri-Rastila is unusual because of its high proportion of **immigrant** children. There are 190 pupils in the school, and nearly half have foreign backgrounds. They speak thirty-three languages alongside Finnish, including Somali, Russian, Turkish, Kurdish, Arabic, and Chinese.

[1] **suburb** *n.* an area where people live together just outside of a city or large town
[2] **corridor** *n.* a hall or passageway in a building
[3] **shriek** *v.* to cry loudly to show emotion such as fear, joy, or surprise
[4] **curriculum** *n.* the subjects making up a course of study in a school
[5] **form** *n.* a grade or a level in school, used especially in British and other European education systems
[6] **compress** *v.* to put or squeeze something into a smaller space

18

READING PREVIEW

A short activity gives students an opportunity to predict the content of the passage to follow. This generates interest in the topic and activates students' background knowledge.

GUIDING QUESTIONS

Questions in the margin encourage students to pause and assess their reading comprehension, annotate the text, and apply critical thinking skills that they have learned.

MAPPING IDEAS

Graphic organizers help students organize the information and ideas they have read and gain familiarity with note-taking and common text organizations.

READING SKILLS WORKSHEETS

A worksheet builds reading skills with activities based on content from the reading. Printed in a handy Skills Workbook to facilitate marking.

Reading 1

MAPPING IDEAS

○ Comprehension

Organize the ideas from Reading 1. Review the passage and fill in the graphic organizer below.

Features of Finland's education system

Student Support	1 _____	Flexibility

- All students get a free 2 _____ and free 3 _____ while they are in school.
- Class sizes tend to be 4 _____

- There is only one 5 _____ that is taken when students are 6 _____.
- Schools give their own tests during 7 _____ to see what needs to be improved.

- Students get to pick 8 _____
- The 9 _____ decides on the subjects, but teachers get to choose 10 _____.

[R W] Before you go on, boost your reading skills. Go to page 174 of the Skills Handbook.

FOCUS ON CONTENT

○ Comprehension

① Circle the main idea of the passage below. For each of the other sentences, check the reason it is not the main idea.

1 Teacher quality is partly responsible for students' academic achievement in Finland.
☐ too general   ☐ too specific   ☐ not in passage   ☐ inaccurate

2 There are sharp differences between the Finnish and the British education systems.
☐ too general   ☐ too specific   ☐ not in passage   ☐ inaccurate

3 The main characteristic of the Finnish learning environment is its flexibility.
☐ too general   ☐ too specific   ☐ not in passage   ☐ inaccurate

4 Finland uses the UK as a model for its education reforms.
☐ too general   ☐ too specific   ☐ not in passage   ☐ inaccurate

20

---

② Mark each statement as true (T), false (F), or inferred (I) according to the passage.

1 Immigrant students that do not speak English must go to private schools in Finland.   T F I

2 Student athletes who go to sports schools in Finland must also get high academic test scores.   T F I

3 Private schools in the UK charge fees, while those in Finland don't.   T F I

4 Primary school teachers get to know their students well because they keep the same classes.   T F I

③ Choose the best answer.

1 What is unique about Meri-Rastila primary school?
a. The principal is also a teacher for fifth and sixth form.
b. The school decided to no longer give the students exams.
c. The school has a large population of immigrant students.
d. It is the first private primary school in Finland.

2 What are the two streams of high schools in Finland?
a. Public and private
b. Academic and vocational
c. Primary and secondary
d. Academic and sports

THINK AND DISCUSS

○ Application

① Read the excerpt from the reading passage.

Finland's Schools Flourish in Freedom and Flexibility

In the corridors at the upper school, teenagers assemble around computer screens picking the classes they will go to for the next few weeks. The school's contemporary building and casually dressed students give it the atmosphere of a new university. Pupils design their own timetables, so teachers get classes made up of new faces every term. However, this flexibility is combined with a rigid approach to the curriculum. While students can decide when they will learn and teachers are free to interpret the subject as they see fit, the school has a long list of compulsory subjects, and the government prescribes exactly what children ought to know in each field.

Discuss the following question with a partner.

- How does the Finnish education system compare with that in your country? What similarities do they share? What differences do they have?

21

FOCUS ON CONTENT

Comprehension questions consolidate and assess students' understanding of the main ideas and key details in the reading.

FOLLOW-UP DISCUSSION

A key passage from the reading serves as the taking-off point for a discussion activity, enabling students to think about and discuss the issues presented in relation to their own lives.

A second, carefully-leveled reading presents a different perspective on the same topic.

Read the passage.

Aiming High: Education and Economic Growth in Singapore

by Jon Maes / Language Cradle Consulting

Singapore is well-known as one of the Four Asian Tigers. Along with Hong Kong, South Korea, and Taiwan, it was given this title because of the country's rapid economic growth over the past fifty years.

Q What is the main point of the passage?

Experts offer a number of explanations for Singapore's rise to riches. One reason they point to is how the country has tied education reforms to the pursuit of national prosperity[1].

Singapore's economy is heavily powered by the shipping industry with its harbor being one of the busiest in the world.

This approach to education has raised Singapore's status for academic excellence. Its students regularly score among the top ten countries according to various research indexes. For example, a survey by the media company Pearson in 2014 ranks Singapore as third in the world for overall education attainment[2]. Only South Korea and Japan scored higher. Also, Singapore placed first for math and second for science in Boston College's 2011 Trends in International Mathematics and Science Study (TIMSS). Even Michael Gove, the UK education minister, has publicly praised Singapore's education methods and quality assurance **mechanisms**. He commented that the UK should look to Singapore as a model for Britain's school reforms.

Q Singapore's education system has received a number of high rankings. How many rankings did the author mention? List them.

So, how exactly has Singapore got ahead of so many other countries? For starters, its government has a strong **commitment** to hiring high-quality teachers. In fact, Singapore had a **shortage**[3] of school staff and **administrators** throughout the 1980s. This brought about policy changes to attract good teachers and retain them by providing them with **ongoing** support. One policy that is proving effective is the GROW package. Introduced in 2007, this $250 million program promotes teachers who display superb[4] standards of instruction. It also rewards teachers who continue with their own **professional** development.

In addition, policy makers work to align[5] the school system with industrial needs. They accomplish this through clear objectives and strict education standards. Like other Asian nations, Singapore has an exam-focused culture. Students are tested at a few points during their school career, and the results are sent to the Ministry of Education (MoE) for **evaluation**. The ministry uses the data as the basis for policy changes and a measure

---

[1] **prosperity** *n.* the state of being wealthy or successful
[2] **attainment** *n.* the act or process of achieving something, especially through work or effort
[3] **shortage** *n.* an amount that is less than what is needed; the state of not having enough
[4] **superb** *adj.* of the finest or highest quality
[5] **align** *v.* to change something to make it match another thing

24

Challenging words and expressions are defined in the text to help students improve comprehension and build their vocabulary.

Reading 2

FOCUS ON CONTENT

① **Choose the best answer.**

1 What is the passage mainly about?
   a. The Ministry of Education's teacher training system in Singapore
   b. The connection between Singapore's education policies and its economic success
   c. How Singapore became a model for education reforms worldwide
   d. The use of technology in Singaporean classrooms

2 What can be inferred from the passage about teachers in Singapore?
   a. Many join the profession only because of the attractive government benefits.
   b. Each one specializes in and teaches more than one academic discipline.
   c. They receive benefits from the government that teachers in many other countries do not get.
   d. All are given a computer or other digital devices when they are hired.

3 Which of the following is a criticism of Singapore's education system that the author mentions?
   a. The schoolwork load is too heavy for students.
   b. There are not enough subjects being taught.
   c. Schools are not giving enough standardized tests.
   d. Lessons need to focus more on job skills.

4 When do Singaporean students first take a national exam?
   a. Only if they are continuing to university
   b. At the end of each grade level
   c. When they are 6 years old
   d. Before they leave primary school

5 Which of the following statements would the author most likely agree with?
   a. The Singaporean government still needs to make a lot of improvements to its schools.
   b. Despite some complaints, Singapore's education system has proven to be successful.
   c. Teachers in Singapore need more training with new technology being invented every year.
   d. Most students in Singapore want to have more control over which classes they take.

② **Complete the sentences with information from the passage.**

1 Singapore is referred to as an _____ because of its economic growth.

2 In Singapore, students in _____ classes often use digital devices to do field research.

3 In 2014, _____ were the only two countries that ranked higher than Singapore for overall education attainment.

4 The GROW package has a budget of _____, with the goal of attracting high-quality teachers.

26

Comprehension questions expose students to a wide range of formats to enhance their test-taking skills.

IDEAS IN ACTION

Talk about the questions with a partner.

1 Which side do you agree with more, the students and parents who criticize the education system in Singapore or the officials in the Ministry of Education? Why?

2 Singapore improved various aspects of its education system, such as teacher quality, technology, and school evaluation. What do you think is the most important aspect of a successful school and why?

CRITICAL THINKING

Recognizing Common Fallacies: Appeal to Authority

One of the most common ways to support a statement or claim is to refer to an expert or authority who makes the same claim. Look at the following example:

> Stephen Hawking says that there must be other planets that support life.
> So, extraterrestrial life must exist in the universe.

When readers encounter this kind of argument, they should ask themselves two questions: First, is the authority cited *really* an authority? In this case, Hawking is a well-respected authority on astrophysics. Second, is the authority *qualified* to comment on the subject in question? In this case, Stephen Hawking's field of expertise is certainly related.

However, there is still a problem with this argument: the truth or falsity of the claim is not related to Hawking's authority. Just because he is an authority, there is no guarantee that the statement is true. In other words, Hawking's authority alone is not enough to make this argument valid. For this reason, although they are commonly used and fairly acceptable, appeals to authority can actually be fallacies.

Answer the questions.

1 You are looking for resources about business trends and globalization. Who would you trust to give the most accurate information? Why?

   a. The owner of a local restaurant
   b. The CEO of a multinational company
   c. The mayor of your city
   d. The computer programmer who lives next door

   _____

2 Which of the following is an example of a false appeal to authority? Why?

   a. A championship-winning basketball coach giving advice about physical fitness
   b. An army general stating that a country is not prepared for war
   c. A famous medical doctor recommending which house to buy
   d. An engineer describing the best way to construct a tunnel

   _____

27

Read the excerpt from Reading 2. There are three appeals to authority in it. Underline them. Then explain whether or not they are credible sources.

> This approach to education has raised Singapore's status for academic excellence. Its students regularly score among the top ten countries according to various research indexes. For example, a survey by the media company Pearson in 2014 ranks Singapore as third in the world for overall education attainment. Only South Korea and Japan scored higher. Also, Singapore placed first for math and second for science in Boston College's 2011 Trends in International Mathematics and Science Study (TIMSS). Even Michael Gove, the UK education minister, has publicly praised Singapore's education methods and quality assurance mechanisms. He commented that the UK should look to Singapore as a model for Britain's school reforms.

_____

_____

_____

VOCABULARY REVIEW

Write the word from the box that can replace the word or phrase in bold in each sentence.

evaluation	credit	ongoing	civil
commitment	professional	administrator	mechanism

1 The new Wimbledon champion _____ her coach with helping her to improve so dramatically.

2 The boss does an annual _____ of each employee's performance for that year.

3 As the _____ of this department, you will be responsible for supervising five employees.

4 He made a _____ to volunteer at the upcoming charity fundraiser.

5 In order to stay competitive, hotels must make _____ efforts to give the best customer service.

6 The soldier injured his hand in the _____ that turns the gun turret.

7 It's a _____ responsibility to vote in government elections.

8 You should hire a _____ contractor to ensure that the job is done properly.

Go to page 175 of the Skills Handbook for the Writing Worksheet.

28

SKILLS WORKBOOK

DEVELOPING READING SKILLS

Lessons and activities in the Skills Workbook help students improve their reading comprehension by focusing on key reading skills.

GUIDED WRITING

A writing worksheet provides guidance and a framework for students to express their own opinion about the topic of the unit.

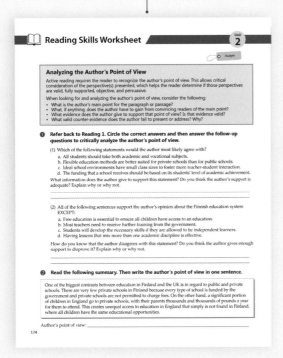

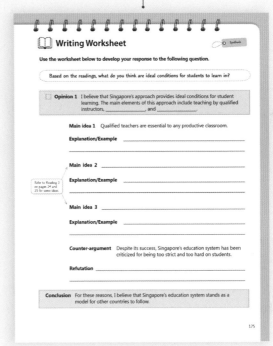

WEBSITE AND MOBILE APP

Get the most out of *On Point* by getting more practice on the dedicated website and mobile app.

- Access code and full instructions at the back of the book
- Log on to **www.compassdigibooks.com** or download the app to your mobile device from Google Play or the Apple App Store
- Extra practice with vocabulary, reading comprehension, listening, and writing
- Get instant feedback on activities, track progress, and submit homework assignments
- Teachers can organize classes, collect homework assignments, and track student progress

ONLINE RESOURCES:
- Answer Key
- MP3 audio recordings of reading passages

UNIT 1

Early Adopters: Leaders or Fools?

The pros and cons of embracing brand-new technology

Think About It

Should people buy new technology as soon as they can?

If you're offered a seat on a rocket ship, don't ask what seat. Just get on.

Sheryl Sandberg

<table>
<tr><td rowspan="2">What you'll learn in this unit:</td><td></td><td>Reading 1 / Early Adopters Fall into a Costly Trap
Reading Skill: Previewing and Predicting</td></tr>
<tr><td></td><td>Reading 2 / The Fun—and the Power—of Being an Early Adopter
Critical Thinking Skill: Detecting Arguments (Premises and Conclusions)</td></tr>
<tr><td>Unit Project</td><td colspan="2">Make Your Point
Express your opinion about being an early adopter of technology</td></tr>
</table>

Before You Read

1 **Read the statements. Check (✔) your response to each statement. Discuss your answers with a partner.**

	Strongly disagree	Disagree somewhat	Agree somewhat	Strongly agree
1. It's kind of embarrassing to have an old cell phone.				
2. I know more about technology than the average person does.				
3. Learning to use a new program or electronic device is fun.				
4. It's worth spending extra money for the best and latest technology.				

2 **Which of the following are you most likely to buy or use right away? Least likely? Discuss your answers with a partner.**

A new social networking site

A new tablet

A new online game

VOCABULARY PREVIEW

Read the sentence. Circle the choice that is closest to the meaning of the AWL word in bold.

1 Don't **underestimate** the costs of being an early adopter.
   a. view as less than it is   b. forget about   c. put off dealing with

2 Some **consumers** want to invest in the latest technology immediately.
   a. experts   b. beginners   c. customers

3 The first versions of a **device** are usually expensive.
   a. program   b. machine   c. game

4 Companies **presumably** want to recover their production costs.
   a. usually   b. likely   c. finally

5 Companies get a lot of their **revenues** from early adopters.
   a. income   b. creativity   c. support

6 After cutting prices, they can **shift** to the next stage of marketing.
   a. add   b. apply   c. move

7 Most customers stayed **neutral**, waiting to see which product would win.
   a. somewhat cautious   b. supporting neither side   c. fairly nervous

8 Which products survive and which die is often **arbitrary**.
   a. not based on reason   b. changing quickly   c. decided in secret

READING PREVIEW

This passage is an article about some of the disadvantages of being an early adopter of technology.

Why might buying a new electronic product as soon as it comes out be a bad idea? Think of at least two reasons and discuss them with a partner.

 Before you go on, boost your reading skills. Go to page 171 of the Skills Handbook.

Track 1

Early Adopters Fall into a Costly Trap

by Brian Ng

It's undeniable: Being among the first to try out a new piece of technology is cool. There's the thrill of doing what has never been done before, the feeling that you're living in the future. And when you're the sole member of your social circle with the latest hot gadget[1], people stare in fascination. They ask you questions. They see you as the holder of powerful, secret knowledge—for a little while, until the next big thing comes along. [5] People tend to **underestimate** the costs of this temporary coolness, which they pay in more ways than one. Don't fall into the early adopter trap. Don't join the first wave of **consumers** who invest in the latest media-hyped hardware; instead, wait and see. In buying electronics, as in most areas of life, delaying gratification[2] is worth it. You will save money and avoid being stuck with defective[3], possibly doomed[4] technology. [10]

C What is the author's main purpose in this passage?
(1) To inform
(2) To persuade
(3) To entertain

To be an early adopter is to throw your money away.

To put it bluntly[5], early adoption is a bad investment. First, the earliest versions of **devices** are not only expensive, they are also the most expensive that those devices will ever be. Companies are **presumably** attempting to recover the cost of production as fast as they can, and they know that there are [15] serious tech-lovers who will pay a great deal to be first. Once the **revenues** from early adopters' purchases are safely in their hands, they can cut the price and **shift** to the next marketing phase: selling the product to everyone else. This is why the cost of the original iPhone dropped about US$200 only eight [20] months after its release. Plus, electronics hardly ever become more expensive because intense competition in the industry puts downward pressure on prices over time. Prices of gadgets will fall shortly after release, and they will likely keep falling. Many new TV models drop significantly in price as little as ten days after hitting the market. Further, electronics rapidly depreciate[6] because they [25] become obsolete[7] so quickly. This means that early adopters pay the maximum price for an item that does not hold onto its value. The resale price of a used cell phone or laptop can drop by fifty percent within just a few months.

Q Underline four numbers in this paragraph. What does each number refer to?

Speaking of becoming obsolete, those who are first to leap into a new technology risk wasting money and time on something that will never catch on. Do you remember [30] high-definition DVDs (HD DVDs)? Neither do a lot of people. In 2006, two competing

---

[1] **gadget** *n.* a device; a useful machine
[2] **gratification** *n.* satisfaction; pleasure
[3] **defective** *adj.* not working properly
[4] **doomed** *adj.* facing certain failure or death

[5] **bluntly** *adv.* briefly and directly
[6] **depreciate** *v.* to become lower in value
[7] **obsolete** *adj.* outdated and no longer in use

formats for high-definition video entered the market: HD DVDs and Blu-ray discs. Both seemed promising, and both required players costing hundreds of US dollars. Cautious consumers decided to stay **neutral**, realizing that one or the other would probably end up dominating and it was difficult to say which. But a few eager consumers rolled the dice[8] and bought an HD DVD player that soon became virtually worthless. For reasons that are not entirely clear—Blu-ray has no obvious technological advantage over its rival—the HD DVD format lost. Sales dropped steadily, and in early 2008 HD DVD players were discontinued. Many new products are similarly doomed to never make it; the early adopters are then stuck with pricey gadgets that do nothing but sit on their shelves collecting dust. And as the story of HD DVD shows, which products survive may be quite **arbitrary**, so even the most knowledgeable among us can be taken by surprise.

Q Why might someone regret purchasing an HD DVD player?

Brand-new products usually have annoying defects.

Another good reason to resist the early-adoption temptation is that the first version of a product typically has defects[9] that cost a lot in time and frustration. For example, when Microsoft's latest game console, Xbox One, was released in 2013, users immediately began to complain of problems. Some of them were malfunctions[10] of the motion sensor while others involved users being unable to get their machines online. Dedicated gamers worked to find and share work-around solutions to these issues. Such problems are so common with new technology that early adopters are basically unpaid beta testers and troubleshooters. Unless this sounds to you like a fun way to spend your time, don't be among the first users. If you wait to learn what the problems are with a new electronic gadget, you can look forward to a smoother experience—or choose a less troublesome product.

Q Why does the author discuss the Xbox One?

Early adopters do something most others are reluctant to do: take on overpriced, insufficiently tested technology for the dubious[11] rewards of being the first and enjoying a short-term increase in status. Learn from their experiences. These trailblazers[12] do the world a service through their willingness to spend extra money and work out the problems with a new product. When other consumers do start using that product, it's cheaper and better—and has a more reliable future. So if you know any early adopters, thank them, and then quietly congratulate yourself on not being one of them.

Q Why should people thank early adopters, according to the reading?

---

[8] **roll the dice** *idiom* to take a risk
[9] **defect** *n.* a flaw; an imperfection
[10] **malfunction** *n.* a failure to work properly

[11] **dubious** *adj.* of questionable worth or quality
[12] **trailblazer** *n.* someone who does something new that others follow

MAPPING IDEAS

Organize the ideas from Reading 1. Review the passage and fill in the graphic organizer below.

The costs of early adoption

First versions of tech products are the most ¹ _____.
- ² _____ in price soon after release
- Quickly lose resale value

Some products never catch on and become obsolete quickly.
- ex.: ³ _____

First versions often have many ⁴ _____.
- ex.: Xbox One
- Early adopters are ⁵ _____ without pay.

FOCUS ON CONTENT

1 **Circle the main idea of the passage below. For each of the other sentences, check the reason it is not the main idea.**

1 The thrill of being first drives early adopters to buy a new product as soon as it is available.
☐ too general   ☐ too specific   ☐ not in passage   ☐ inaccurate

2 Early adopters buy expensive, possibly worthless products that need more testing.
☐ too general   ☐ too specific   ☐ not in passage   ☐ inaccurate

3 Being an early adopter of technology doesn't make sense.
☐ too general   ☐ too specific   ☐ not in passage   ☐ inaccurate

4 Early adopters often have to deal with products that do not work properly yet.
☐ too general   ☐ too specific   ☐ not in passage   ☐ inaccurate

2 **Complete the sentences with information from the passage.**

1 Companies set prices high at first because they want to _____
_____.

2 Competition in the tech industry means that prices _____
_____.

3 Used electronics lose their resale value fast because _____
_____.

4 After finding problems with the Xbox One, devoted gamers _____
_____.

3 **Choose the best answer.**

1 What does the author imply about early adopters in paragraph 1?
   a. They tend to be fairly wealthy.
   b. They are fully aware of the costs of early adoption.
   c. They do not pay much attention to the media.
   d. They enjoy impressing others.

2 According to paragraph 3, which of the following is true about HD DVDs?
   a. It is not clear why consumers chose Blu-ray discs over them.
   b. It is possible that they will become popular again in the future.
   c. Their sales fell steadily starting in 2008.
   d. They were technologically better than Blu-ray discs.

THINK AND DISCUSS

 Application

1 **Read the excerpt from the reading passage.**

Early Adopters Fall into a Costly Trap

When Microsoft's latest game console, Xbox One, was released in 2013, users immediately began to complain of problems. Some of them were malfunctions of the motion sensor while others involved users being unable to get their machines online. Dedicated gamers worked to find and share work-around solutions to these issues.

Discuss the following questions with a partner.

• Think of another new technology that was problematic for its first users. Did you personally experience these problems? Did users find solutions?

• How often do you get frustrated when using technology? What do you do about it? Give an example.

② **A friend asks you which laptop to buy for schoolwork: a new model with lots of unique extra features or a year-old used one with only basic features. What advice would you give your friend? Write a short explanation of your answer.**

_____

_____

_____

_____

_____

VOCABULARY REVIEW

Fill in the blanks with the correct words from the box. Change the form of the word if necessary.

revenue	presumably	arbitrary	neutral
consumer	device	shift	underestimate

1 A new _____ allows users to watch any TV channel on their computers.

2 I was late because I _____ how long the trip would take by subway.

3 Switzerland is known for remaining _____ in times of war.

4 The company's annual report shows a nine-percent increase in _____.

5 Many newspapers today are _____ their focus to online content.

6 _____, most businesses will be closed on the national holiday.

7 Be a smart _____; don't be fooled by advertising tricks.

8 The judge's decision confused and angered us because it seemed _____.

Reading 2

VOCABULARY PREVIEW

Match each AWL word in bold with its meaning from the box.

a. done by one's own choice	b. to ask for help or advice	c. not directly expressed
d. special skill or knowledge	e. a job	f. a reason for doing something
g. a task or project	h. allowing things to happen without changing them	

_____ **1** Buying an unfamiliar gadget can be a difficult **undertaking** for some people.

_____ **2** Early adopters don't **passively** use new technology but experiment with it.

_____ **3** Economic status is probably a **motive** for many early adopters to buy the latest technology.

_____ **4** Having the latest gadget makes people feel that they possess technological **expertise**.

_____ **5** For IT professionals, it could help their careers to be the first to buy technology that is related to their **occupation**.

_____ **6** Their colleagues can **consult** them when they have a tech-related question.

_____ **7** Asking for input from early adopters was Google's way of **implicitly** flattering them.

_____ **8** Early adopters know that they are **voluntary** test subjects when they buy new technology.

READING PREVIEW

This passage is an article about why some people enjoy being early adopters.

This graph shows how consumers are divided into early adopters, the majority, and laggards (latecomers) when it comes to new technology.

Discuss with a partner:

• Where do you usually fall on this graph? Why?
• Why do you think some people like being early adopters?

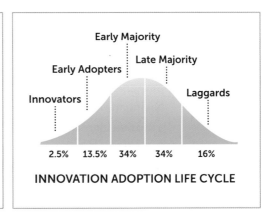

INNOVATION ADOPTION LIFE CYCLE

The Fun—and the Power—of Being an Early Adopter

Track 2

by Marie Lavoisier

If you are not an early adopter, you almost certainly know one. She was the first person in your group of friends to own a smart phone, and she couldn't wait to show you what it could do. He was the guy who talked excitedly about moving all his data to the cloud before you even knew what the cloud was. Early adopters are that minority of users who adopt a new technology in its earliest days before it is widely used or even thoroughly tested. According to one widely cited piece of research, early adopters are defined as the first thirteen percent or so of people who begin using a device, game, social network, or other new product. While the majority of us sit back and wait for an innovation to prove itself, the early adopters jump right in. By doing so, they get the pleasure of conquering a new frontier[1], enhanced prestige[2], and even power within the tech industry. [10]

Q Underline the main idea of this passage.

For many people, trying to figure out a new and unfamiliar piece of technology is a slightly scary **undertaking**. For early adopters, it's a favorite way to spend their time. They get a deep sense of satisfaction from learning and playing with new technology. By definition, early adopters have an unusual interest in (and, usually, skill at using) new technology, so they don't just **passively** follow instructions. They love to throw away the user's guide and experiment. Jimmy Selix, who blogs

Early adopters love the freedom to discover new ways of using technology.

about being an early adopter, says that people like him would look at something new and say to themselves, "This is going to . . . " or "I can use this for . . . " or "What if I . . . ?" As pioneers[3], the first users of a product get to discover ways of using it, including some that even its makers haven't thought of.

Q What is one way in which early adopters are different from other people? Underline the information.

Perhaps even more fun than becoming the master of a new technology is sharing that [25] mastery with others and enjoying the respect that goes along with it. When it comes to having the newest electronic device, surely a superficial[4] concern with economic status is a **motive** for many early adopters—after all, most first-generation devices are expensive. But a desire for status as a tech whiz[5] is more defensible and useful. As one early buyer of the first-generation iPad explained, "It gives you an air of **expertise** in technological [30]

---

[1] **frontier** *n.* a new area of study or activity
[2] **prestige** *n.* respect and admiration
[3] **pioneer** *n.* someone who opens up a new line of thought or activity; a trailblazer

[4] **superficial** *adj.* shallow; without substance
[5] **whiz** *n.* a genius; an expert

matters to have the latest gadget." When the price of the device does drop, many of the early adopter's friends, family, and social media contacts will want one, too. And guess who will happily give them help and advice? Early adopters are more knowledgeable about technology than most of those around them are, and they are justly[6] proud of that. A well-earned reputation as an expert obviously has other benefits as well. Always being up-to-date on the latest program or IT service relevant to your **occupation**—and being the person that all your colleagues **consult** when they have a tech question—cannot exactly hurt your career.

Q Underline two benefits of early adoption mentioned in this paragraph.

Besides, as the earliest and savviest[7] consumers of new technology, early adopters wield[8] a great deal of influence in the industry. The most obvious way they exercise this influence is to point out bugs and other defects to the makers of the new product, who then quickly fix them. But more than that, social media has given early adopters a forum to discuss new products and make a name for themselves as shapers of public opinion. "Companies are now starting to

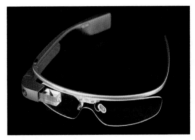

Early adopters help shape the development of new products, such as Google's wearable computer.

realize that . . . early adopters are more than just geeks with a passion but also a great way to spread their brand and products," writes Selix. As a result, the first purchasers of a product are often rewarded with discounts, free lifetime service, or other incentives[9] for good reviews. They also sometimes have a say in up-and-coming products. For example, in 2012 Google began the Glass Explorer program. "Explorers" chosen according to their influence were given the chance to buy Glass, the wearable computer, before it became available in stores, and to help shape the product's development. Later, Google invited the public to apply for the Explorer program, saying applicants would be judged in part on how creative, original, and influential their suggested uses for Glass were. This is a clever way to **implicitly** flatter[10] early adopters, get their ideas, and make use of their prestige, all at the same time.

Q Circle four ways in which companies reward early adopters.

Early adopters realize that they are, in a sense, **voluntary** guinea pigs[11], but they are OK with that. For them, figuring out a new tablet or game or web app has its own charm. It allows them to learn something new and employ their creativity. It improves their

---

[6] **justly** *adv.* deservedly; rightly
[7] **savvy** *adj.* clever; knowledgeable about something
[8] **wield** *v.* to have and use

[9] **incentive** *n.* a reward designed to motivate
[10] **flatter** *v.* to praise, especially out of self-interest
[11] **guinea pig** *n.* an experimental subject; a person being experimented on

status as technological experts in their social circle. And it gives them influence with tech companies, who crave[12] their input and approval. Increasingly, technology is the driver of change in the world. Who wouldn't want to be one of the people who drive change in technology?

65

C Is the author's point of view on early adopters positive, negative, or neutral?

---

[12] **crave** *v.* to want strongly

Reading 2

FOCUS ON CONTENT

1 **Choose the best answer.**

○ Comprehension

1 What is the main idea of paragraph 2?
   a. Early adopters enjoy experimenting with new technology.
   b. Early adopters tend to have a lot of technical expertise.
   c. Early adopters are good at teaching others to use technology.
   d. Early adopters usually ignore instruction manuals.

2 Which of the following is true, according to paragraph 3?
   a. Early adopters dislike advising their friends and family on technology.
   b. Early adopters like being viewed as experts.
   c. No early adopters are motivated by a desire to appear rich.
   d. Most early adopters are not as knowledgeable as they seem.

3 According to paragraph 3, early adoption can help a career because _____.
   a. it makes the adopter attractive to tech companies
   b. it means the adopter is always working with the best devices
   c. it makes the adopter appear wealthy and successful
   d. it gives the adopter a reputation for technical knowledge

4 According to paragraph 4, what are the effects of social media? (Choose two answers.)
   a. It allows companies to persuade people to be early adopters.
   b. It allows early adopters to influence public opinion.
   c. It has led companies to view early adopters as a marketing tool.
   d. It has made it easier for early adopters to contact each other.

5 What can be inferred from paragraph 4?
   a. The incentives that companies give to early adopters are unethical.
   b. People in the Glass Explorer program are mainly early adopters.
   c. Early adopters generally give good reviews to new devices.
   d. Some of the Explorers will probably be hired by Google.

2 **Check the statements that are true according to the passage. Correct the false statements.**

1 ☐ Early adopters invent new uses for products.

_____

2 ☐ When early adopters report bugs, companies don't respond.

_____

3 ☐ Early adopters sometimes get discounts or free repairs.

_____

4 ☐ The first Google Explorers were chosen at random.

_____

IDEAS IN ACTION

Talk about the questions with a partner.

1 Besides an interest in technology, what traits do you think early adopters tend to have in common?

2 Would you be willing to praise a product in social media in exchange for a discount or other rewards? Why or why not?

CRITICAL THINKING

Detecting Arguments (Premises and Conclusions)

Arguments are not always clearly stated as such. It's a very important critical thinking skill to be able to recognize arguments and think about them separately without being influenced by other techniques that the writer may use to try and convince you, such as exaggeration or emotional language.

Start by picking out the **conclusion** of the argument—the statement that is being supported. There are some key words that might help you identify the conclusion: _therefore, thus, hence, so, consequently_, and _this shows that_.

Next, identify the **premises** (or reasons) given to support the conclusion. Some key words that indicate a premise are _as, because, since, given that, for, on the grounds that_, and _this follows from_. There may be some statements supporting the final conclusion that are, in turn, supported by other statements. These other statements are known as subarguments. Also, there may be unstated premises. Try to think of all of the reasons that are needed to make an argument that is complete and makes sense.

13

Read the arguments from Reading 2. Then identify each sentence as a premise (P) or a conclusion (C).

1

(1) By definition, early adopters have an unusual interest in (and, usually, skill at using) new technology, so they don't just passively follow instructions. (2) They love to throw away the user's guide and experiment . . . (3) As pioneers, the first users of a product get to discover ways of using it, including some that even its makers haven't thought of.

(1) _____   (2) _____   (3) _____

2

(1) Besides, as the earliest and savviest consumers of new technology, early adopters wield a great deal of influence in the industry. (2) The most obvious way they exercise this influence is to point out bugs and other defects to the makers of the new product, who then quickly fix them. (3) But more than that, social media has given early adopters a forum to discuss new products and make a name for themselves as shapers of public opinion.

(1) _____   (2) _____   (3) _____

VOCABULARY REVIEW

Write the word from the box that can replace the word or phrase in bold in each sentence.

occupation	consult	voluntary	implicitly
undertaking	expertise	passively	motive

1 There were no clear threats; instead, threats were made _____ in the letter.

2 Decorating this huge apartment will be an enormous _____.

3 The public is no longer willing to _____ accept the government's abuses.

4 It's quite common for people to work in the same _____ as their parents did.

5 If you experience side effects from this medication, _____ your doctor.

6 The extra class is _____, but I strongly encourage everyone to attend.

7 Simple greed is the _____ for a great many crimes.

8 My friend's mechanical _____ comes in handy whenever my car breaks down.

Go to page 172 of the Skills Handbook for the Writing Worksheet.

UNIT
2

Focus on Learning

Different kinds of education systems from around the world

Think About It

What are the ideal conditions
for students to learn in?

Education is the most powerful weapon which you
can use to change the world.

Nelson Mandela

Unit Project | **Make Your Point**
Discuss the ideal conditions for student learning

Before You Read

1 **Look at the following aspects of school learning environments and add another of your own. Then rank them from 1 (most important) to 6 (least important). Compare and discuss your rankings with a partner.**

_____ Qualified teachers

_____ Technology in the classroom

_____ Interesting textbooks

_____ Tutoring help for assignments and tests

_____ Useful facilities such as a library and a gym

_____ _____
(your idea)

2 **Answer the questions. Discuss your answers with a partner.**

1 What type of schoolwork do you like most? What do you like least?
   a. Group projects
   b. Written essays
   c. Presentations
   d. Tests
   e. Other (specify)

2 Is there anything you would change about your school if you could? Why?

Reading 1

VOCABULARY PREVIEW

Read the sentence. Circle the choice that is closest to the meaning of the AWL word in bold.

1 Teachers are allowed to **interpret** the subject they are teaching in their own way.

    a. avoid   b. forget   c. explain

2 Children **commence** primary school studies when they turn 7 years old.

    a. pass   b. start   c. allow

3 Most Finnish children attend **comprehensive** schools, which serve every kind of student, rather than the more selective private schools.

    a. all-inclusive   b. difficult   c. high-quality

4 Finland's success is **attributable to** the importance that is given to teaching.

    a. caused by   b. blamed on   c. improved by

5 The **contemporary** building makes the school look like a new university.

    a. large   b. modern   c. expensive

6 These alternative schools do not charge fees and are **subsidized** by the government.

    a. taxed   b. managed   c. given money

7 You can see students **assemble** around computers to pick their next classes.

    a. work   b. fighting   c. gather

8 That school is known to have a high number of **immigrant** children.

    a. talented   b. newcomer from abroad   c. happy

READING PREVIEW

This passage is an article about schools in Finland. The author discusses what is special about the Finnish education system.

> Schools are under a lot of pressure to provide a quality education. How do people judge a school's level of success? What positive outcomes must schools show? Think of a few ways that schools are evaluated and share them with a partner.

Track 3

Finland's Schools Flourish in Freedom and Flexibility

by Jeevan Vasagar

At Meri-Rastila primary school in a suburb[1] of Helsinki, pupils shake the snow off their boots in the corridors[2], then peel them off and shuffle softly into class in socks. After a 45-minute lesson, they are out in the playground again.

The Finnish school day is short and intermixed with bursts of running around, shrieking[3], and sledding outdoors. Children **commence** their studies when they are older, the year 5 they turn 7, and there is no pressure on them to do anything academic before then.

Q What is the main idea of the article? Underline it.

The Finnish education system contrasts sharply with that of England. Every Finnish child gets a free school meal and a free education, which extends to the university level.

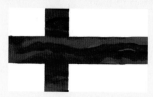

Finland is a country of 5.4 million people, with about 600,000 students from primary to secondary school.

There are no league tables, no school inspections, and only one set of national exams, which children take at age 18 10 when they are about to leave school. The government only conducts the national assessments to sample the population as a means of keeping track of school performance, but these results are not made public.

Meri-Rastila's principal, Ritva Tyyska, said, "I think it's quite 15 good that they don't rank the schools because we have good teachers, we have a curriculum[4], and we have to obey it. In every school, we teach about the same things. The methods can be a little bit different, [but you] get the same education.

"We have these tests in the fifth or sixth form[5] that are the same tests at each and 20 every school. We get the results, and we see where we stand. But that is not common knowledge. And if it's not good, we have to check what we are doing wrong, what we have to improve."

In Finland, the state decides what should be taught, but not how. If they like, teachers can take their children outside for "wood mathematics," where they go into the nearest 25 patch of forest and learn to add and subtract by counting twigs or stones in the open air.

A typical lesson compresses[6] several disciplines into one. In a combined class, children who don't speak Finnish as their first language are taught to identify and name the parts of a mouse and then mark on a chalk outline of the country where the animal lives. It is a literacy lesson, but a biology and geography one as well. 30

Meri-Rastila is unusual because of its high proportion of **immigrant** children. There are 190 pupils in the school, and nearly half have foreign backgrounds. They speak thirty-three languages alongside Finnish, including Somali, Russian, Turkish, Kurdish, Arabic, and Chinese.

---

[1] **suburb** *n.* an area where people live together just outside of a city or large town

[2] **corridor** *n.* a hall or passageway in a building

[3] **shriek** *v.* to cry loudly to show emotion such as fear, joy, or surprise

[4] **curriculum** *n.* the subjects making up a course of study in a school

[5] **form** *n.* a grade or a level in school, used especially in British and other European education systems

[6] **compress** *v.* to put or squeeze something into a smaller space

Rami Salminen begins his class on the Roman Empire by hauling[7] out a boy for tossing a book at a classmate. It is the last hour of the school day, and he decides to give a very traditional lesson, focusing on the textbook and having students write down key passages rather than inviting a debate. This class is a relatively big one, with twenty-six children. But as a rule, classes in Finnish schools tend to be small, and teachers usually keep the same classes as students move through primary school, which allows teachers to get to know the children well.

Salminen said, "That's the best way; you know the pupils, you know their special needs, and you get to know their parents as well. Many parents can't do their job properly, and they [the children] need an adult understanding, listening to them, trying to help and encourage them."

Q What is Rami Salminen's opinion of his students' parents?

Finland's success is **attributable**, in part, to the high status of teaching. Reforms in the 1980s transferred teacher training to universities and required every teacher to have a master's degree.

In the corridors at the upper school, teenagers **assemble** around computer screens picking the classes they will go to for the next few weeks. The school's **contemporary** building and casually[8] dressed students give it the atmosphere of a new university. Pupils design their own timetables, so teachers get classes made up of new faces every term. However, this flexibility is combined with a rigid approach to the curriculum. While students can decide when they will learn and teachers are free to **interpret** the subject as they see fit, the school has a long list of compulsory[9] subjects, and the government prescribes exactly what children ought to know in each field.

Q How is Finnish upper school both flexible and rigid? Underline the information.

The most striking difference between the Finnish system and the British is the fact that the vast majority of Finnish children attend **comprehensive** schools. The country does have a handful of faith-based and alternative schools that are legally private, but they cannot charge fees, and they are **subsidized** by the state. However, these private schools are permitted to set their own catchment[10] areas. Meanwhile, 7.2 percent of children in England attend private schools, which are free to select pupils and charge fees. A private education costs parents an average of £10,100 a year.

Q What does the author say is the biggest contrast between Finnish and British education systems?

Timo Lankinen, director general of the Finnish national board of education, said, "Somehow we have had that kind of social agreement that basic education in Finland should be provided for all, and take all levels into account, and somehow parties in Finland have accepted it. If it [remains] this way, there isn't any need for private schools."

Instead, there is diversity within the state system, with high schools allowed to select pupils on the basis of academic merit after 16. There are two separate streams for post-16 education: academic schools and vocational[11] ones, although both can lead to higher education.

Mäkelänrinne is one of thirteen schools in the country that specialize in sports, picking its students on the basis of their sporting records as well as academic test scores. While the school is state-run and accessible to all, its ambition is to help develop a sporting elite[12]. In the Olympic-size pool it shares with the local community, divers cut sharply into the water as their coach points out a 19-year-old in a black swimsuit. "She's the best female diver in Finland at the moment," the coach said. "Her goal is London [2012]."

---

[7] **haul** *v.* to pull or carry with force
[8] **casually** *adv.* done without a lot of planning; not formally
[9] **compulsory** *adj.* required or necessary; mandatory
[10] **catchment** *n.* an area from which something is collected, in this case, students
[11] **vocational** *adj.* relating to an education that trains students for specific jobs
[12] **elite** *n.* a group of people

MAPPING IDEAS

Comprehension

Organize the ideas from Reading 1. Review the passage and fill in the graphic organizer below.

Features of Finland's education system

Student Support	1 _____	Flexibility
• All students get a free 2 _____ and free 3 _____ while they are in school. • Class sizes tend to be 4 _____	• There is only one 5 _____ that is taken when students are 6 _____. • Schools give their own tests during 7 _____ to see what needs to be improved.	• Students get to pick 8 _____. • The 9 _____ decides on the subjects, but teachers get to choose 10 _____.

R W Before you go on, boost your reading skills. Go to page 174 of the Skills Handbook.

FOCUS ON CONTENT

Comprehension

1 **Circle the main idea of the passage below. For each of the other sentences, check the reason it is not the main idea.**

1 Teacher quality is partly responsible for students' academic achievement in Finland.

☐ too general ☐ too specific ☐ not in passage ☐ inaccurate

2 There are sharp differences between the Finnish and the British education systems.

☐ too general ☐ too specific ☐ not in passage ☐ inaccurate

3 The main characteristic of the Finnish learning environment is its flexibility.

☐ too general ☐ too specific ☐ not in passage ☐ inaccurate

4 Finland uses the UK as a model for its education reforms.

☐ too general ☐ too specific ☐ not in passage ☐ inaccurate

② **Mark each statement as true (T), false (F), or inferred (I) according to the passage.**

1 Immigrant students that do not speak English must go to private schools
in Finland.   T F I

2 Student athletes who go to sports schools in Finland must also get high
academic test scores.   T F I

3 Private schools in the UK charge fees, while those in Finland don't.   T F I

4 Primary school teachers get to know their students well because they keep
the same classes.   T F I

③ **Choose the best answer.**

1 What is unique about Meri-Rastila primary school?

    a. The principal is also a teacher for fifth and sixth form.
    b. The school decided to no longer give the students exams.
    c. The school has a large population of immigrant students.
    d. It is the first private primary school in Finland.

2 What are the two streams of high schools in Finland?

    a. Public and private
    b. Academic and vocational
    c. Primary and secondary
    d. Academic and sports

THINK AND DISCUSS

Application

① **Read the excerpt from the reading passage.**

Finland's Schools Flourish in Freedom and Flexibility

In the corridors at the upper school, teenagers assemble around computer screens picking the classes they will go to for the next few weeks. The school's contemporary building and casually dressed students give it the atmosphere of a new university. Pupils design their own timetables, so teachers get classes made up of new faces every term. However, this flexibility is combined with a rigid approach to the curriculum. While students can decide when they will learn and teachers are free to interpret the subject as they see fit, the school has a long list of compulsory subjects, and the government prescribes exactly what children ought to know in each field.

Discuss the following question with a partner.

- How does the Finnish education system compare with that in your country? What similarities do they share? What differences do they have?

② **Write a short response to the following questions.**

- The passage discusses the high level of flexibility in the Finnish education system. Do you think this form of flexibility is a good idea? Why or why not?
- What problems could arise if an education system was given too much flexibility?

VOCABULARY REVIEW

Fill in the blanks with the correct words from the box. Change the form of the word if necessary.

comprehensive	assemble	subsidize	interpret
commence	immigrant	contemporary	attributable

1 They were born here, but their parents are _____ from China.

2 Poor performance is usually _____ to lack of effort, not lack of ability.

3 The company needs a(n) _____ marketing plan that promotes all of their products.

4 They don't understand English. Could you _____ for us?

5 We are asking the university to _____ more student activities this term, if there is enough money in the budget.

6 The instructions show the steps for how to _____ the wooden table.

7 I heard that her new job will _____ at the beginning of next month.

8 He prefers _____ music to classical music.

Reading 2

VOCABULARY PREVIEW

Match each AWL word in bold with its meaning from the box.

> a. having to do with the activities of citizens
> b. dedication to someone, something, or an action
> c. to give approval or praise for something done
> d. a study of something in order to judge or measure it
> e. a person that manages a business, organization, or institution
> f. continuing
> g. of or having to do with a certain job or work
> h. a process or system that is used to produce a particular result

_____ **1** The government conducts **evaluations** to see how well students are learning.

_____ **2** Experts **credit** Singapore's economic success to its education system.

_____ **3** To do their job effectively, teachers need **ongoing** assistance from the government.

_____ **4** The government makes a **commitment** to raise the quality of teachers in order to improve school education.

_____ **5** Teachers will receive financial support if they get extra training or other forms of **professional** development.

_____ **6** Students need to learn **civil** literacy because it teaches them how to participate in society.

_____ **7** Singapore is recognized for having effective **mechanisms** for monitoring students' academic progress.

_____ **8** The country lacked school **administrators** at the time.

READING PREVIEW

This passage is about the education system in Singapore. The author describes how the Singaporean government manages its schools.

Based on your knowledge, what aspects of Asian education systems in general might the author talk about? Make a list and share with your partner.

Aiming High: Education and Economic Growth in Singapore

Track 4

by Jon Maes / Language Cradle Consulting

Singapore is well-known as one of the Four Asian Tigers. Along with Hong Kong, South Korea, and Taiwan, it was given this title because of the country's rapid economic growth over the past fifty years.

Q What is the main point of the passage?

Experts offer a number of explanations for Singapore's rise to riches. One reason they point to is how the country has tied education reforms to the pursuit of national prosperity[1].

This approach to education has raised Singapore's status for academic excellence. Its students regularly score among the top ten countries according to various research indexes. For example, a survey by the media company Pearson in 2014 ranks Singapore as third in

Singapore's economy is heavily powered by the shipping industry with its harbor being one of the busiest in the world.

the world for overall education attainment[2]. Only South Korea and Japan scored higher. Also, Singapore placed first for math and second for science in Boston College's 2011 Trends in International Mathematics and Science Study (TIMSS). Even Michael Gove, the UK education minister, has publicly praised Singapore's education methods and quality assurance **mechanisms**. He commented that the UK should look to Singapore as a model for Britain's school reforms.

Q Singapore's education system has received a number of high rankings. How many rankings did the author mention? List them.

So, how exactly has Singapore got ahead of so many other countries? For starters, its government has a strong **commitment** to hiring high-quality teachers. In fact, Singapore had a shortage[3] of school staff and **administrators** throughout the 1980s. This brought about policy changes to attract good teachers and retain them by providing them with **ongoing** support. One policy that is proving effective is the GROW package. Introduced in 2007, this $250 million program promotes teachers who display superb[4] standards of instruction. It also rewards teachers who continue with their own **professional** development.

In addition, policy makers work to align[5] the school system with industrial needs. They accomplish this through clear objectives and strict education standards. Like other Asian nations, Singapore has an exam-focused culture. Students are tested at a few points during their school career, and the results are sent to the Ministry of Education (MoE) for **evaluation**. The ministry uses the data as the basis for policy changes and a measure

---

[1] **prosperity** *n.* the state of being wealthy or successful

[2] **attainment** *n.* the act or process of achieving something, especially through work or effort

[3] **shortage** *n.* an amount that is less than what is needed; the state of not having enough

[4] **superb** *adj.* of the finest or highest quality

[5] **align** *v.* to change something to make it match another thing

of school performance. It then commends[6] schools whose students are doing well and requires improvements of schools whose students aren't.

Besides localized[7] tests for each class, students take national exams at specific grade
35 levels. The first is the Primary School Leaving Examination after six years of primary school. At the secondary level, most schools in Singapore follow the British system by using the Cambridge curriculum. This means that students take a General Certificate of Education (GCE) Ordinary Levels exam when they are 15 to 16 years old. Then, they take a GCE Advanced Levels exam at ages 17 to 18 as they exit high school and continue on
40 to university.

Another important feature of Singapore's school system is the adoption of digital devices. It is common to find a classroom full of tablets or laptops equipped with education programs and games for student learning. You are also likely to see a science teacher with a group of students off campus using tablets or other digital devices to do field
45 research[8]. The widespread use of technology is intended to give students more chances to collaborate with their peers, as part of the MoE's plans to move away from the heavy focus on high-pressure testing.

Q What is the attitude of some Singaporean students and parents toward the education system in their country?

However, not everyone is happy with the structure of the education system or the changes that the government is trying to make. The MoE receives criticism from both
50 students and parents that school is still too demanding and that the government relies too much on standardized tests. They also want more to be done to develop important competencies[9] such as creative thinking and public speaking.

In response, officials point out that the education system is rather flexible. There are a variety of options offered across disciplines[10], including schools for sports and the arts. In
55 addition, since 2010, students are required to be taught skills such as **civil** literacy, global awareness, and responsible decision-making.

Since it became a nation in 1965, Singapore has undergone major economic progress. There can be little doubt that this success is due in large part to its education system. Singapore's growth can be **credited** to the many policy reforms concentrated on
60 equipping students with the skills they need to succeed in today's job markets. To achieve this end, schools are required to employ qualified teachers. Furthermore, the MoE holds schools accountable[11] through regular performance reviews. All of these actions arise from Singapore's competitive drive to be among the world's best.

Q The author mentions three reasons for the success of Singapore's education system. Underline them.

6   **commend** v. to praise or give credit
7   **localized** adj. confined to a particular place or area
8   **field research** n. the collecting of information outside of a school, laboratory, or work setting
9   **competency** n. a skill or ability that a person has

10 **discipline** n. an area or subject of academic study
11 **accountable** adj. responsible for providing an explanation or justification, especially for one's own actions

Reading 2

FOCUS ON CONTENT

Comprehension

① **Choose the best answer.**

1 What is the passage mainly about?
   a. The Ministry of Education's teacher training system in Singapore
   b. The connection between Singapore's education policies and its economic success
   c. How Singapore became a model for education reforms worldwide
   d. The use of technology in Singaporean classrooms

2 What can be inferred from the passage about teachers in Singapore?
   a. Many join the profession only because of the attractive government benefits.
   b. Each one specializes in and teaches more than one academic discipline.
   c. They receive benefits from the government that teachers in many other countries do not get.
   d. All are given a computer or other digital devices when they are hired.

3 Which of the following is a criticism of Singapore's education system that the author mentions?
   a. The schoolwork load is too heavy for students.
   b. There are not enough subjects being taught.
   c. Schools are not giving enough standardized tests.
   d. Lessons need to focus more on job skills.

4 When do Singaporean students first take a national exam?
   a. Only if they are continuing to university
   b. At the end of each grade level
   c. When they are 6 years old
   d. Before they leave primary school

5 Which of the following statements would the author most likely agree with?
   a. The Singaporean government still needs to make a lot of improvements to its schools.
   b. Despite some complaints, Singapore's education system has proven to be successful.
   c. Teachers in Singapore need more training with new technology being invented every year.
   d. Most students in Singapore want to have more control over which classes they take.

② **Complete the sentences with information from the passage.**

1 Singapore is referred to as a(n) _____ because of its economic growth.

2 In Singapore, students in _____ classes often use digital devices to do field research.

3 In 2014, _____ were the only two countries that ranked higher than Singapore for overall education attainment.

4 The GROW package has a budget of _____, with the goal of attracting high-quality teachers.

IDEAS IN ACTION

Talk about the questions with a partner.

1 Which side do you agree with more, the students and parents who criticize the education system in Singapore or the officials in the Ministry of Education? Why?

2 Singapore improved various aspects of its education system, such as teacher quality, technology, and school evaluation. What do you think is the most important aspect of a successful school and why?

CRITICAL THINKING

> ## Recognizing Common Fallacies: Appeal to Authority
>
> One of the most common ways to support a statement or claim is to refer to an expert or authority who makes the same claim. Look at the following example:
>
> > Stephen Hawking says that there must be other planets that support life. So, extraterrestrial life must exist in the universe.
>
> When readers encounter this kind of argument, they should ask themselves two questions: First, is the authority cited *really* an authority? In this case, Hawking is a well-respected authority on astrophysics. Second, is the authority *qualified* to comment on the subject in question? In this case, Stephen Hawking's field of expertise is certainly related.
>
> However, there is still a problem with this argument: the truth or falsity of the claim is not related to Hawking's authority. Just because he is an authority, there is no guarantee that the statement is true. In other words, Hawking's authority alone is not enough to make this argument valid. For this reason, although they are commonly used and fairly acceptable, appeals to authority can actually be fallacies.

1 **Answer the questions.**

    1 You are looking for resources about business trends and globalization. Who would you trust to give the most accurate information? Why?

        a. The owner of a local restaurant
        b. The CEO of a multinational company
        c. The mayor of your city
        d. The computer programmer who lives next door

        _____

    2 Which of the following is an example of a false appeal to authority? Why?

        a. A championship-winning basketball coach giving advice about physical fitness
        b. An army general stating that a country is not prepared for war
        c. A famous medical doctor recommending which house to buy
        d. An engineer describing the best way to construct a tunnel

        _____

2 **Read the excerpt from Reading 2. There are three appeals to authority in it. Underline them. Then explain whether or not they are credible sources.**

> This approach to education has raised Singapore's status for academic excellence. Its students regularly score among the top ten countries according to various research indexes. For example, a survey by the media company Pearson in 2014 ranks Singapore as third in the world for overall education attainment. Only South Korea and Japan scored higher. Also, Singapore placed first for math and second for science in Boston College's 2011 Trends in International Mathematics and Science Study (TIMSS). Even Michael Gove, the UK education minister, has publicly praised Singapore's education methods and quality assurance mechanisms. He commented that the UK should look to Singapore as a model for Britain's school reforms.

_____

_____

_____

VOCABULARY REVIEW

Write the word from the box that can replace the word or phrase in bold in each sentence.

evaluation	credit	ongoing	civil
commitment	professional	administrator	mechanism

1 The new Wimbledon champion _____ her coach with helping her to improve so dramatically.

2 The boss does an annual _____ of each employee's performance for that year.

3 As the _____ of this department, you will be responsible for supervising five employees.

4 He made a _____ to volunteer at the upcoming charity fundraiser.

5 In order to stay competitive, hotels must make _____ efforts to give the best customer service.

6 The soldier injured his hand in the _____ that turns the gun turret.

7 It's a _____ responsibility to vote in government elections.

8 You should hire a _____ contractor to ensure that the job is done properly.

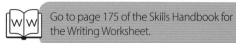
Go to page 175 of the Skills Handbook for the Writing Worksheet.

The Evolving Workplace

Rethinking what makes employees happy and successful

I ♥ my job

Think About It

What can companies do to make working conditions better for employees?

The magic formula that successful businesses have discovered is to treat customers like guests and employees like people.

Tom Peters

What you'll learn in this unit:

Reading 1 / Breaking Free of 9 to 5
Reading Skill: Asking Questions While Reading

Reading 2 / How Companies Can Keep Their Talent
Critical Thinking Skill: Identifying Deductive and Inductive Arguments

Unit Project | **Make Your Point**
Express your opinion about how companies can make conditions better for employees

Before You Read

1 **Answer the questions. Discuss your answers with a partner.**

1 At what time of day do you work or study best?
   a. Early morning   b. Midday   c. Afternoon   d. Evening

2 Do you think working from home would suit you?
   a. Yes   b. No

3 Do you think employees should stay loyal to their companies?
   a. Yes, because that's the best way to get job security.
   b. Yes, but only if the company treats them well.
   c. No, they should always be on the lookout for a better job.

4 If you could change one of the following about how a typical office works in your country, what would it be?
   a. More flexible hours   b. More respect for employees
   c. More benefits (health insurance, pension plan, etc.)

2 **If you could have only one of the following benefits in your job, which would you choose? Why? Discuss with a partner.**

A

Bonuses for good ideas

B

Plenty of time off

Reading 1

VOCABULARY PREVIEW

Read the sentence. Circle the choice that is closest to the meaning of the AWL word in bold.

1 Some people are most **energetic** in the morning.
   a. cheerful
   b. active
   c. relaxed

2 The reasons for adopting the forty-hour workweek might **justify** not getting rid of it.
   a. cause to end
   b. make necessary
   c. provide a good reason for

3 Henry Ford **instituted** a five-day workweek in his factories.
   a. invented
   b. established
   c. rejected

4 Gradually, governments started to **legislate** working hours.
   a. put into law
   b. research
   c. have debates about

5 An eight-hour workday became the **convention** in the business world.
   a. custom
   b. goal
   c. strategy

6 People who like to sleep late are not necessarily **unmotivated**.
   a. not cooperative
   b. not good at one's job
   c. not ambitious

7 People are **incapable** of changing their biological clock.
   a. not interested
   b. not able
   c. not knowledgeable

8 There were several reasons for our **eventual** switch to flexible hours.
   a. agreed-upon
   b. gradual
   c. later

 Before you go on, boost your reading skills. Go to page 177 of the Skills Handbook.

READING PREVIEW

This passage is an article about the usual 9 to 5 workday. The author discusses how it began and why it should change.

What is one advantage of having everyone in a company work the same hours in the same place? What is one disadvantage? Discuss your ideas with a partner.

Breaking Free of 9 to 5

by Jim Edwards

When we started our own company, my partners and I just assumed that we'd keep regular office hours. Every other job any of us had ever had was like that. Why would ours be any different?

However, it quickly became clear that things weren't going to play out¹ that way. The thing is that, like many developers, I'm a night owl². I don't get going until about noon, and I'm at my most productive³ between 8 p.m. and midnight. My co-founders are the complete opposite; they're most **energetic** first thing in the morning, and by mid-afternoon, they're ready to crash. For the first three months, we all struggled—I with the morning meetings, they with my late-night phone calls. Forcing everyone to work on the same schedule quickly proved to be an exercise in frustration. We just weren't being as productive as we could be, and we all knew it.

Q How is the author different from his co-founders?

The problems our fledgling⁴ startup faced made us examine our assumptions about our working hours. Why do most people work a 9-to-5 day, five days a week? A quick look at the history of working hours reveals just how outdated our current standard is.

That Was Then, This Is Now

The current workday emerged almost a hundred years ago, in a different era. However, if there were good reasons for it—reasons that still apply today—then perhaps that could **justify** not abandoning it.

Well, the fact is that there were never very convincing reasons for adopting the forty-hour workweek. During the 1920s, the Industrial Revolution was in full swing. Factories typically ran twenty-four hours a day, with workers putting in ten- to sixteen-hour shifts. Then, Ford Motor Company founder Henry Ford **instituted** a five-day, forty-hour workweek in his factories but still paid his workers the same wages. Surprisingly, it wasn't his intention to improve his workers' quality of life, their health, or even their productivity. Ford later explained in interviews that he had made the change to a forty-hour workweek to give workers more time to shop—specifically, to buy his cars. Regardless of the motivation, other manufacturers followed suit⁵ and more workers started demanding the same conditions. Gradually, governments started **legislating** the forty-hour workweek as part of labor law. The 9-to-5 workday soon became the **convention** in almost all industries.

Q What change did Henry Ford make? Why did he make it?

You no longer have to be in the office to be productive.

At the time, a uniform work schedule for everyone did make some sense. After all, the office was the locus⁶ of work, and workers had to be available during work hours to collaborate⁷ in person. There were no other options. However, in the era of laptops, cell phones, ubiquitous⁸ wireless connectivity, and cloud solutions, do arguments for this model really carry any weight? If workers can work from anywhere at any time, why

---

¹ **play out** *phrasal v.* to develop; to become in the end
² **night owl** *n.* a person who likes to stay up late
³ **productive** *adj.* working hard and getting a lot done
⁴ **fledgling** *adj.* newly formed and still developing

⁵ **follow suit** *idiom* to do the same as
⁶ **locus** *n.* a central place; a site where something happens
⁷ **collaborate** *v.* to work together on something
⁸ **ubiquitous** *adj.* found everywhere; very common

should they have to come in to the office at 9 and leave at 5? Beyond the occasional face-to-face meeting, there seems to be no justification for having all workers follow the same schedule. The forty-hour workweek definitely seems outdated.

Night Owls in an Early-Bird World

The conventional workday is ideal for one type of person in particular: the early bird[9]. Research shows that genetic factors determine the length of a person's circadian cycle, the series of biochemical signals that influence the body's rise and fall in energy levels and trigger drowsiness, wakefulness, hunger, etc. This cycle determines whether someone is an early bird or a night owl, according to Katherine Sharkey, a professor at Brown University and the associate director of the Sleep for Science Research Lab. If your cycle is a bit shorter, you're most likely an early bird and the 9-to-5 routine suits you just fine. When you come in to work in the morning, you're all fired up and ready to go; and by the end of the day, your energy level starts to drop off.

But what if, like a sizable[10] proportion of the population, you are more productive later in the day or even at night? The 9-to-5 routine forces night owls to try to be productive at times when their alertness and energy level are lowest. As a result, night owls typically get a reputation for being lazy or **unmotivated**. This is unfair, given that they are merely victims of their own wake-sleep cycle, which they are more or less **incapable** of changing. However, if given the chance to work on a schedule that better suits them, night owls can be just as productive as early birds and may actually outperform[11] them.

Breaking from Tradition

When my co-founders and I sat down to re-evaluate our approach to working hours, the change was an easy sell. But the mental shift to the new approach didn't come naturally. Even now, three years later, I still find myself checking the time periodically[12] through the day, particularly in the late afternoon, and calculating how many more hours I should put in. On days when I work less than eight hours, I have to admit that I still feel a bit guilty—like I'm not working as hard as I could or that I'm cheating someone. But on another level, I'm well aware that this way of thinking is wrong.

Several steps led to our company's **eventual** break from the traditional 9-to-5 schedule. Originally, we adopted a flextime system. Everyone had to be at the office between 11 a.m. and 3 p.m., beyond which they could just come and go as they liked, provided they worked a full eight hours a day. However, flextime was abandoned after a few months, too. The quantitative measure of how many hours someone worked just wasn't as important to us as the qualitative aspect. We wanted beautiful, creative products and brilliant solutions to problems, and we found we got more of those out of our team when we let them set their own schedules.

Now our work schedules are guided by our energy levels and the specific projects we have to get done. Instead of forcing ourselves to be productive at certain times, we can all customize our schedule to ideally suit our individual lifestyles. We care not about how many hours we work, but about what we do in those hours.

On the surface, having no set working hours might seem like a recipe for disaster, but for our company it's been perfect. Since abandoning a set work schedule, we've seen improvements in our productivity, the quality of our work, our health, and the overall quality of our lives. It's a decision we've never regretted, and it's one I would recommend other business owners give some serious thought to.

---

9   **early bird** n. a person who likes to get up early
10 **sizable** adj. fairly large
11 **outperform** v. to perform better than
12 **periodically** adv. from time to time

C Circle the term that is defined in this paragraph. Underline the definition.

C Summarize the argument in this paragraph.

Q Why did the company eventually abandon flextime? Underline the information.

MAPPING IDEAS

 Comprehension

Organize the ideas from Reading 1. Review the passage and fill in the graphic organizer below.

Breaking free of the 9-to-5 workday

History:

1920s, Industrial Revolution: people worked

1 _____

Forty-hour workweek: started by Henry Ford; became the

2 _____

Made sense before Internet

Why it should change:

Cell phones and Internet allow people to work anywhere, anytime

Circadian cycle: genetically determined

3 _____ not productive in the morning

After the change:

4 _____ to make the mental shift

Work guided by energy levels; quality more important than quantity

Improvements in

5 _____

No regrets about the decision

FOCUS ON CONTENT

Comprehension

1 **Circle the main idea of the passage. For each of the other sentences, check the reason it is not the main idea.**

1 The 9-to-5 workday may have been necessary in the past, but it has become outdated.

☐ too general ☐ too specific ☐ not in passage ☐ inaccurate

2 Factories run two separate shifts in order to suit early birds and night owls.

☐ too general ☐ too specific ☐ not in passage ☐ inaccurate

3 Studies show that workers can get just as much done even if they work shorter hours.

☐ too general ☐ too specific ☐ not in passage ☐ inaccurate

4 To adapt to modern times and individual needs, companies should switch to customized schedules.

☐ too general ☐ too specific ☐ not in passage ☐ inaccurate

2 **Check the statements that are true according to the passage. Correct the false statements.**

1 When the author's company started, only he had trouble with the schedule.

_____

2 Ford started the forty-hour workweek so that his employees would be more productive.

_____

3 Night owls make up a very small part of the population.

_____

4 The author's company tried flextime before it switched to customized schedules.

_____

3 **Choose the best answer.**

1 What is the main idea of paragraph 6?
   a. Technology allows people to do their jobs wherever they want.
   b. Changes in technology have removed the need for a 9-to-5 workday.
   c. Nowadays, it is rare for all the workers in an office to have the same schedule.
   d. Cell phones and computers mean people no longer communicate face-to-face.

2 What can be inferred about the author and his co-workers from paragraphs 10–11?
   a. They all have fairly similar habits and lifestyles.
   b. They are working fewer hours per week than before.
   c. They are having trouble adjusting to the new system.
   d. They work more hours on some days than on others.

THINK AND DISCUSS

Application

1 **Read the excerpt from the reading passage.**

Breaking Free of 9 to 5

Now our work schedules are guided by our energy levels and the specific projects we have to get done. Instead of forcing ourselves to be productive at certain times, we can all customize our schedule to ideally suit our individual lifestyles. We care not about how many hours we work, but about what we do in those hours.

Discuss the following questions with a partner.

- Why might some people think this system seems like "a recipe for disaster," as the author puts it?
- Think of the type of job you have or intend to have someday. Would a customized schedule like this be possible and effective for you? Why or why not?

2 **Night owls and early birds need different work schedules. How do you think other individual differences affect employees' needs in the workplace? Choose one pair from the boxes or think of your own. Briefly explain what employers can do to accommodate both types.**

• Likes to work quietly at the desk OR • **Likes** social interaction and physical activity

_____

_____

_____

• Assertive and confident OR • Shy and nervous about speaking up

_____

_____

VOCABULARY REVIEW

Fill in the blanks with the correct words from the box. Change the form of the word if necessary.

convention	justify	incapable	eventual
unmotivated	energetic	institute	legislate

1 Gloria did poorly at school and seemed _____, so her parents offered her rewards for good grades.

2 I was sleepy when I got up, but I felt more _____ after a quick jog.

3 _____ against junk food is a silly idea because the government can't control people's eating habits.

4 Being in a bad mood does not _____ treating other people poorly.

5 The company announced that it is _____ a new, stricter dress code.

6 My grandmother went against _____ by becoming a lawyer in the 1950s, when very few women did so.

7 Babies are _____ of holding their heads up until they are about a month old.

8 Despite their _____ loss, the team played a magnificent game.

VOCABULARY PREVIEW

Match each AWL word in bold with its meaning from the box.

a. an effect; a consequence
b. a sphere of influence or control
c. amazing; remarkable
d. showing deep understanding
e. to change to suit different conditions
f. a large company
g. possibly
h. the condition of being more important; priority

_____ **1** Google sets an example for other **corporations** in terms of how they treat their employees.

_____ **2** These expenses can **potentially** avoided if companies can keep their employees.

_____ **3** Companies have to think of **insightful** ways of keeping employees happy.

_____ **4** There are some **implications** of these practices that some employees might not like.

_____ **5** People's personal lives sometimes take **precedence** over their work.

_____ **6** Some companies provide **phenomenal** benefits to employees.

_____ **7** Google keeps its employees' creative ideas safely within its **domain**.

_____ **8** If they are careful, these companies will **adapt** to these conditions and survive.

READING PREVIEW

This passage is an article about why people leave their jobs and what companies can do to keep them.

What do you think are the major reasons people are unsatisfied with their jobs? Think of at least two and discuss them with a partner.

How Companies Can Keep Their Talent

by Kelly Shepherd / Language Cradle Consulting

Track 6

C What does the author compare employee happiness to?

Today's labor force possesses considerable expertise. And yet, it is no secret that those who are dissatisfied in their current position will look for opportunities to join a different company that might offer them more. To ensure and sustain their success, companies need to work hard at keeping their talented employees happy. After all, a house is only as strong as its foundation, and the foundation of a company is the well-being and satisfaction of its employees. 5

However, holding on to a loyal workforce can be challenging. There are aggressive recruiters[1] out there who have no problem stealing other companies' top performers. They lure potential employees with promises of high salaries, supportive work environments, and profit-sharing plans. 10

A company's best people can be stolen by its rivals.

Thus, the critical issue for executives is how to reduce their company's turnover rate[2]. According to an article by the Center for American Progress, "it costs businesses about one-fifth of a worker's [annual] salary to replace that worker. For businesses that experience high levels of turnover, this 15 can add up to represent significant costs that can **potentially** be avoided by implementing[3] workplace flexibility and earned sick days at little or no cost at all." So it is extremely important for companies to think of **insightful** approaches to keep their employees happy. 20

Q According to the passage, how does a high turnover rate affect a company?

Q Underline the benefits that Google employees receive.

For eleven years in a row, Google has been first on *Fortune* magazine's list of 100 top companies to work for. The benefits of employment with Google include free food and clothing, on-site health care, laundry services, a gymnasium, and free haircuts, among other things. Also, in the unfortunate event of an employee dying, his or her legal partner is entitled[4] to fifty percent of the worker's income for one decade. In terms of the working 25 conditions, compensation package, and perks it offers, Google is exemplary[5].

However, there are also **implications** of Google's employment practices that might prompt[6] employees to move elsewhere. For example, there are overqualified workers who have grown tired of what they see as menial[7] labor. A former employee lists providing tech support for Google ad products, manually taking down flagged content from YouTube, 30 and writing basic software to test the color of a button on the website as reasons for leaving. These people have studied at some of the most prestigious institutions in the world only to be given uninspiring work. And since all employees in a workplace like Google have excellent educations and are generally adept at doing what they do, there is little opportunity to move up the ladder[8]. 35

[1] **recruiter** *n.* someone who finds people for a company to hire

[2] **turnover rate** *n.* the frequency with which people leave a company and are replaced

[3] **implement** *v.* to put into effect

[4] **entitle** *v.* to have the right to

[5] **exemplary** *adj.* extremely good and deserving to be admired

[6] **prompt** *v.* to cause

[7] **menial** *adj.* boring and unimportant

[8] **move up the ladder** *idiom* to advance to higher job positions within a company

Then there is the question of work-life balance. Evidently, some wage-earners at Google feel as though they have lost their autonomy[9] in the process of working for Google. An anonymous former employee describes "spending the
40 majority of your life eating Google food, with Google co-workers . . . you eventually lose sight of what it's like to be independent of the big G." It is possible that Google has lost track of the bigger picture in that workers are also individuals. Employees have their own lives and interests
45 outside the office, which sometimes take **precedence** over

Employers have to remember that work isn't everything.

work. There are exceptions. For example, Amrita Kohli, a writer for New Dehli Television, wrote about how a little girl had asked Google to let her father have one day off besides Saturday. The girl wanted to be with her dad for his birthday. To their credit, Google complied with this request by granting the man an entire week off.

50 Vacation allowance is not the only policy that Google has looked at revising. In January of 2013, Farhad Manjoo, a columnist for *Slate* Magazine, wrote about Google's workplace practices and argued that Google's ability to keep its female staff needed to be improved upon. When the human resources department investigated, they discovered that women were quitting because they were given inadequate maternity leave. So Google changed
55 its policy to make it more attractive for women to stay. It increased its maternity leave from three months to five. And when these women return from their leave, they can work part-time until they feel comfortable coming back full-time.

Even though companies like Google provide **phenomenal** benefits, there still seems to be a huge gap between profits and profit-sharing. When successful ideas are generated
60 by employees, should those employees not also share in the financial rewards above and beyond their salaries? Yet, under Google's current model, an individual employee's work is company property. By providing perks[10] and benefits, Google strives to keep its staff's brilliant ideas safely within its **domain**. However, although the employees use tools provided by Google, the company does not own the employees' minds. It does not own
65 the passion or the creativity of its workers. This may be something Google should look into. After all, Twitter was founded by Evan Williams, and Instagram by Kevin Systrom, both former employees of Google. And if Google does not improve its employee retention[11] rate, a future former employee might well start the next big thing on the Internet.

Google is still an excellent company to work for. And it has extensively modified its
70 employee retention strategies. For the success of the business, Google and other similar companies should set an example for other **corporations** by investing in their employee pool. It is through their talent as innovators that these companies will **adapt** and survive well into the future.

Q Underline the quote in this paragraph. How does that person feel?

C What is the author's opinion about Google in this paragraph?
(1) It should encourage its employees to start their own companies.
(2) It should share its profit with its employees.

---

9 **autonomy** *n.* independence
10 **perk** *n.* (short for *perquisite*) something good given to an employee in addition to pay

11 **retention** *n.* the continued keeping or use of something

39

FOCUS ON CONTENT

1 **Choose the best answer.**

1 What is the main idea of paragraph 4?
   a. Google attracts the most talented people in the field.
   b. Workers at Google have no reason to complain.
   c. Google does many things to keep employees happy.
   d. Most employees at Google say they like working there.

2 According to paragraph 5, what are two possible disadvantages of working at Google?
   a. Long hours
   b. Lack of benefits
   c. Few chances for promotion
   d. Dull tasks

3 According to paragraph 6, Google responded to a little girl's request by _____.
   a. throwing her father a birthday party
   b. giving her father a job
   c. raising her father's salary
   d. giving her father extra time off

4 We can infer from paragraph 7 that the author _____.
   a. agrees with Farhad Manjoo's opinion
   b. thinks Google does not hire enough women
   c. thinks everyone should have the option to work part-time
   d. disagrees with Google's current maternity leave policy

5 What does the author imply about Evan Williams and Kevin Systrom in paragraph 8?
   a. They owe most of their wealth and success to Google.
   b. They quit Google so they could profit from their own ideas.
   c. They probably made a mistake by leaving Google.
   d. They are examples of how Google dominates its employees' lives.

2 **Complete the sentences with information from the passage.**

1 Recruiters sometimes try to steal other companies' _____.

2 If a Google employee dies, his or her partner receives _____.

3 The people that Google hires are unusually _____.

4 Maternity leave at Google now lasts for _____.

IDEAS IN ACTION

Talk about the questions with a partner.

1 Do you think you would like working at Google? Why or why not?

2 Besides the ideas discussed in the passage, how else can companies reward and keep their top-performing employees?

CRITICAL THINKING

Identifying Deductive and Inductive Arguments

Arguments are either deductive or inductive. A **deductive argument** is one in which the conclusion *necessarily* follows from the premises, as in this example:

> (1) If a company treats its employees well, it can keep talented people on staff.
> (2) Google treats its employees well.
> (3) Therefore, Google can keep talented people on staff.

Inductive arguments are somewhat different. Their conclusion is not logically certain. Inductive arguments only show that something is probably true or at least likely.

> (1) A few large companies have started offering new fathers time off from work.
> (2) So, it's likely that this is a trend that will eventually catch on with all companies.

There are many types of inductive arguments. Some make a general statement about a group that is based on information about some members of that group. Other inductive arguments use trends, evidence, authority, or causal relationships to show the probability of something being true. Their strength or weakness depends on many factors; generally speaking, though, if the premises are fairly reliable and can be generalized, it's quite likely that the conclusion is reasonable. For example, the following inductive argument is very weak.

> (1) Google provides free laundry service to its employees.
> (2) So, it's likely that many other large tech companies will also start doing this.

Even though the premise is true, it's unreasonable to generalize it as this argument does.

Look at the following arguments based on Reading 2. Check the correct type of argument.

1
> (1) It is more expensive for companies to hire new workers than to keep their existing ones.
> (2) When given two options, companies should choose the cheaper one.
> (3) Thus, companies should try to keep their existing workers.

☐ Deductive   ☐ Inductive

2

(1) Google gives its employees free food and clothing.
(2) Google provides its employees with health care and a gym.
(3) Google is a good employer.

☐ Deductive   ☐ Inductive

3

(1) Google used to offer limited maternity leave.
(2) Google had trouble keeping its female employees.
(3) Google changed its maternity leave policy.
(4) Google changed its maternity leave policy in order to keep its female employees.

☐ Deductive   ☐ Inductive

VOCABULARY REVIEW

Fill in the blanks with the correct words from the box. Change the form of the word if necessary.

potentially	precedence	corporation	insightful
adapt	phenomenal	domain	implication

1 The theory of evolution says that species _____ to survive in their environments.

2 This candidate is well-educated and smart, but she has no experience working for a large _____.

3 The article includes a very _____ discussion of why people love having pets.

4 Before quitting your job, you have to consider the financial _____.

5 In the future, self-driving cars will _____ make the roads safer.

6 My roommate does the cooking and cleaning, but repairs are my _____.

7 When plans with friends conflict with your study schedule, your studies take _____.

8 Richard is only so-so at playing the piano, but he's a _____ guitarist.

Go to page 178 of the Skills Handbook for the Writing Worksheet.

UNIT 4

The Future Is Now

How new technology could improve the quality of life

Think About It

What technology might have the greatest impact on society in the future?

Any sufficiently advanced technology is indistinguishable from magic.

Arthur C. Clarke

Unit Project | **Make Your Point**
Express your opinion about what technology will impact humans the most

Before You Read

1. **In your opinion, which of the following have experienced the greatest changes from technology in the past twenty-five years? Rank them from 1 (greatest change) to 6 (least change). Compare and discuss your rankings with a partner.**

_____	Transportation	_____	Medicine and medical equipment
_____	Communications	_____	Education
_____	Food production	_____	Entertainment

2. **With a partner, decide what new technologies your country's research funds would be best spent on. Explain your opinion.**

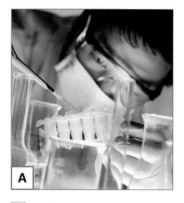

A

☐ Medical research

B

☐ Innovative transportation

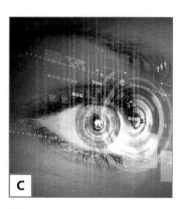

C

☐ Other technology (specify)

VOCABULARY PREVIEW

Read the sentence. Circle the choice that is closest to the meaning of the AWL word in bold.

1 The **coordinator** of the institute might have the solution to the problem of side effects from chemotherapy.

    a. owner   b. doctor   c. director

2 Nanotubes release their load of medicine when they are **adjacent** to their target.

    a. in a straight line   b. close   c. moving

3 The European Union's ObservatoryNano has been **assigned** an important task.

    a. officially given   b. in discussion on   c. contracted to do

4 ObservatoryNano supports decision makers through its **analysis** of trends in nanoscience.

    a. approval   b. examination   c. creation

5 The organization has published a report on the **ethics** of nanotechnology.

    a. morality   b. difficulty   c. usefulness

6 There is no clear **distinction** between medical devices and pharmaceuticals.

    a. connection   b. difference   c. problem

7 It is not easy to determine what **regulations** should be applied to medical products.

    a. research   b. theories   c. laws

8 The confusion regarding these issues could be **resolved** by the end of the year.

    a. opened up   b. talked about   c. sorted out

READING PREVIEW

This passage is an article about using nanotechnology for treating diseases.

> Nanotechnology means technological tools that are extremely small. With a partner, guess how this might relate to medical treatments.

Track >

Nanotechnology World: Nanomedicine Offers New Cures

by Alok Jha
© 2011, Guardian News & Media Ltd. Used by permission.

The human body is a great nanoscale[1] engineer. Cells push and pull billions of molecules around every second in order to grow, communicate with each other, attack germs, or heal after injury. This activity is managed at a macro- (or system-) scale by key organs, including the brain. But it always relies on the rules of physics and chemistry. The rules are coded within these biomolecules and apply at the nanoscale. This feat of automatic engineering is usually known by a more familiar name: biology.

Interpreting, copying, and controlling biology in a bid[2] to make lives healthier and happier is one of the aims of the modern nanoscientist. One way of doing this is to detect the possible development of disease. Nanoscience will provide better tools to look for the molecular clues that could signal problems before they occur.

Q What is one goal of nanoscience? Underline it.

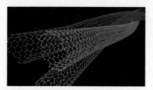

Scientists now create tiny molecules that glow different colors to help locate cancer cells.

Engineers at Ohio State University, for example, have invented polymeric nanoparticles[3] stuffed with even smaller particles of semiconductors (tiny computer chips called "quantum dots"). These particles shine with different colors depending on the molecules they are attached to. The resulting complex nanoparticles can glow red, yellow, and green. This can then allow scientists to track the movements of, say, a range of molecules in a cancer cell under a microscope. Scientists could use these nanoparticles to observe the development of a cancer at the molecular level. This, in turn, could give them key insights into how to stop or treat the disease.

Once a virus or disease is diagnosed[4], getting drugs into people in the most effective way is extremely important. Take cancer treatment. Chemotherapy usually involves a combination of toxic drugs, which kill the cancer cells but also damage normal tissues. It is almost impossible, therefore, to have effective cancer therapy without serious side-effects such as hair loss, nausea[5], or problems with bone marrow.

Q Conventional chemotherapy has a number of negative side effects. Circle them.

Alfred Cuschieri, **coordinator** of the Institute for Medical Science and Technology at Dundee and St. Andrews universities might have the solution. He recently finished working on the NINIVE project, a new way of using carbon nanotubes that are designed to copy a biological virus. Each nanotube carries a pharmaceutical[6] payload[7] on its surface. This tiny structure is able to get into a specific cell type—cancerous or otherwise—much like a nanosized needle. When the nanotubes are directly **adjacent** to their target, a pulse of microwaves from the outside causes them to release their loads inside the cells. "It is coated to make it biocompatible[8]," said Cuschieri, "and we developed side chains on the surfaces onto which we can attach the drugs we want to attach. It becomes basically a carrier."

---

[1] **nanoscale** *adj.* extremely small; microscopic

[2] **in a bid to (do something)** *phrase* in an attempt to do something

[3] **polymeric nanoparticle** *n.* a microscopic plastic particle

[4] **diagnose** *v.* to determine what illness is affecting a person

[5] **nausea** *n.* a feeling of being sick and wanting to vomit

[6] **pharmaceutical** *adj.* related to medicines; *n.* a medicine

[7] **payload** *n.* something that is carried, usually by a vehicle or missile

[8] **biocompatible** *adj.* able to be accepted by the body and not attacked by the immune system

The NINIVE system has already been proven in experiments on mice. It should be possible to attach any drug or molecule to the nanotubes. Once injected into a patient, the drug carriers would wander through the bloodstream until their payload is released by the external microwave pulse. This would only happen at the site of a cancer or other area of interest. Thus, the side effects from any toxic drugs would be reduced. "My guess is that targeted drug delivery systems based on carbon nanotubes will probably start to be tested in early studies in about three to four years' time," says Cuschieri.

Q How do cancer treatment by chemotherapy and treatment by nanomedicine differ? Name two ways.

The next step after treatment of a disease is to rebuild the tissue that has been lost. Again, nano-engineering can help. In 2008, John Kessler, a biologist, and Samuel Stupp, a biomaterials engineer, both at Northwestern University, Chicago, developed a nano-engineered gel to help nerve cells regrow. Inject the gel at the site of a backbone injury, and it self-assembles into a "scaffold[9]"—a physical structure that supports new nerve fibers as they grow up and down the spinal cord, the group of nerves within the backbone. The results were published in the *Journal of Neuroscience*. They showed that after six weeks of tests in mice with spinal injuries, the animals could use their hind legs to walk again.

"There is no magic bullet or one single thing that solves the spinal cord injury. But this gives us a brand-new technology to be able to think about treating this disorder," says Kessler. "It could be used in combination with other technologies, including stem cells, drugs, or other kinds of interventions[10]."

These are exciting developments. But it's worth considering the wider effects of nanotechnology. More and better tests could result in increased treatment of actually healthy people or simply raise general anxiety in the wider population about their health. It seems silly to stop medical advances that could prevent pain and suffering for millions of people, but progress must be open and accountable to the public.

C What can be inferred from this paragraph?
(1) Some doctors are unethical.
(2) Tests can give false positive results.

The EU ObservatoryNano is **assigned** an important job in this regard. The organization supports European policy makers through scientific and economic **analysis** of nanoscience and nanotechnology developments. It has produced a report on the **ethics** of nanotechnology written by Ineke Malsch, director of Malsch TechnoValuation. She says the problem with regulating medical nanotechnology can be how to define a product's area of application. "The **distinction** between a medical device and a pharmaceutical is quite fuzzy. It's not so easy to find out which **regulations** should be applicable to a particular product."

How do you regulate a drug-releasing implant[11], for example? Is Cuschieri's nano-carrier a pharmaceutical or a medical device? A key issue, says Malsch, is the lack of common international agreement of what a nanoparticle is and what constitutes a nanomedicine. "There is continuing discussion about these definitions, which will hopefully be **resolved** before the end of the year."

Current regulations are enough for current technologies, says Malsch, but she adds that this will need to be reviewed. However, over-regulating now would also be a mistake. Pre-empting[12] (and trying to pre-regulate) technology that does not yet exist isn't a good idea, she says.

This view was backed by Professor Andrew Maynard, director of the Risk Science Center, who says, "With policy makers looking for clear definitions on which to build 'nano-regulations,' there is a growing danger of science being pushed aside."

---

[9] **scaffold** *n.* a temporary structure for holding workers and materials while a building is being built

[10] **intervention** *n.* a medical treatment, especially one to stop the spread of a disease

[11] **implant** *n.* something that is put into the human body, traditionally through surgery

[12] **pre-empt** *v.* to prevent something from occurring by taking some action

MAPPING IDEAS

Comprehension

Organize the ideas from Reading 1. Review the passage and fill in the graphic organizer below.

Nanomedicine: new cures and new challenges

Cures

- For tracking ¹ _____ at molecular level:

  Nanoparticles stuffed with semiconductors used to observe development of ² _____

- As targeted drug delivery system:

  Carbon ³ _____ designed to carry disease-fighting pharmaceuticals

- For rebuilding tissue:

  Nano-engineered gel used as "scaffold" to support growth of new ⁴ _____

Challenges

- Problems in determining difference between medical devices and ⁵ _____
- ⁶ _____ of industry could hurt science.

R W Before you go on, boost your reading skills.
Go to page 179 of the Skills Handbook.

FOCUS ON CONTENT

Comprehension

1 Circle the main idea of the passage below. For each of the other sentences, check the reason it is not the main idea.

1 Engineers can now make tiny objects called nanoparticles.

☐ too general   ☐ too specific   ☐ not in passage   ☐ inaccurate

2 The inventor of the first nanotube became a very wealthy man.

☐ too general   ☐ too specific   ☐ not in passage   ☐ inaccurate

3 The EU ObservatoryNano organization regulates all nanoscience in Europe.

☐ too general   ☐ too specific   ☐ not in passage   ☐ inaccurate

4 Nanoscience presents amazing cures as well as problems in the medical field.

☐ too general   ☐ too specific   ☐ not in passage   ☐ inaccurate

② **Choose the best answer.**

1 What can be inferred about the function of the "quantum dots" mentioned in paragraph 3?

    a. They release cancer-fighting medicine.

    b. They hold polymeric nanoparticles inside them.

    c. Microwaves make them glow red, yellow, or green.

    d. They do not attack and destroy cancerous cells.

2 How does paragraph 5 relate to paragraph 4?

    a. Paragraph 5 contrasts two drug therapies, and paragraph 4 compares them.

    b. Paragraph 5 provides an illustrative example of a disease described in paragraph 4.

    c. Paragraph 5 suggests a way of overcoming a problem presented in paragraph 4.

    d. Paragraph 5 describes a drawback of a cancer treatment introduced in paragraph 4.

③ **Mark each statement as true (T) or false (F) according to the passage.**

_____ **1** A special covering makes nano-engineered devices compatible with the human body.

_____ **2** The NIVINE system will be approved for general use in three or four years' time.

_____ **3** Nano-engineered gel could be used to correct serious spinal injuries.

_____ **4** ObservatoryNano drafted an ethical code on nanomedicine for doctors to follow.

_____ **5** There is not a good definition of nanomedicines at this time.

THINK AND DISCUSS

① **Read the excerpt from the reading passage.**

Nanotechnology World: Nanomedicine Offers New Cures

Interpreting, copying, and controlling biology in a bid to make lives healthier and happier is one of the aims of the modern nanoscientist. One way of doing this is to detect the possible development of disease. Nanoscience will provide better tools to look for the molecular clues that could signal problems before they occur.

Discuss the following questions with a partner.

- What other illnesses do you think could be treated with nanotechnology?
- How could nanotechnology cure these illnesses?

2 **You are in charge of the budget at a large medical research facility. In your opinion, which of the following would be the best use of your research facility's funds? Write a short explanation.**

Curing cancer

Curing physical disabilities

Curing everyday illnesses

_____

_____

_____

VOCABULARY REVIEW

Choose the best words to fill in the blanks.

1 Our office is located directly _____ to a major highway.
a. adjacent   b. compatible   c. assigned

2 The leaders of the two countries met in order to _____ their differences.
a. coordinate   b. resolve   c. assign

3 The young man questioned the _____ of his company's business practices.
a. technologies   b. ethics   c. regulation

4 Each student is _____ a teacher who will act as his or her adviser throughout the year.
a. analyzing   b. pre-empting   c. assigned

5 There are clear _____ between traditional and modern medicine.
a. resolutions   b. interventions   c. distinctions

6 After a careful _____ of the problem, the scientist developed an effective solution.
a. analysis   b. coordination   c. implementation

7 The _____ of the program was chosen because of her rare combination of education and experience.
a. diagnosis   b. coordinator   c. analysis

8 Although passed with good intentions, many environmental _____ simply lead to further problems later.
a. ethics   b. assignments   c. regulations

VOCABULARY PREVIEW

Match each AWL word in bold with its meaning from the box.

a. a model
b. at the same time
c. a government department
d. to guess what will happen and prepare
e. to admit
f. as a result
g. a situation involving several factors
h. early

_____ **1** Traffic accidents will decrease, and **consequently** the number of traffic deaths will drop.

_____ **2** The writer **acknowledges** that self-driving cars are likely to be on the road in the future.

_____ **3** **Preliminary** estimates suggest that self-driving cars would save many lives each year.

_____ **4** The National Highway Traffic Safety **Administration** states that self-driving cars would reduce traffic jams.

_____ **5** The cars can **anticipate** braking and accelerating, so they will use less gas.

_____ **6** Self-driving cars have the ability to perform several actions **concurrently**.

_____ **7** Self-driving cars are an entirely new automotive **paradigm**.

_____ **8** Traffic deaths would drop after removing human mistakes from the **equation**.

READING PREVIEW

This is a letter to the editor in which the author responds to a newspaper article criticizing self-driving cars.

We may soon see self-driving vehicles on our roads. What advantages might these vehicles have over traditional cars? Think of two ideas and discuss them with a partner.

Track 8

Drive My Car . . . Please

by Jon Maes / Language Cradle Consulting

C Why does the author quote Donald Blaise?

Normally, I'm 100 percent supportive of the acclaimed[1] columnist Donald Blaise's innovative and sometimes unusual ideas. But reading his recent article "Just Say 'No' to Self-driving Cars," I was surprised by his argument against this exciting new technology. How could a champion[2] of new ideas be against self-driving cars? Though he **acknowledges** that their use in the future is very likely, he goes on to write: "Self-driving cars are a terrible idea because a human being has no control over the vehicle!"

Well, Donald, that's kind of the point, don't you think? Self-driving cars are actually a fantastic idea because they will do exactly what the name implies—they'll handle the driving for you! When the car takes control, the driver will be safer, freer, and happier. Blaise's explanation for why self-driving cars are terrible is exactly why they're so amazing.

C Besides statistics, what does the author use to support his opinion about self-driving cars?
(1) Personal experience
(2) Research findings
(3) Expert opinion

Mr. Blaise, as it turns out, does most of his work from home. He doesn't have to sit in his car every morning and afternoon, moving slowly along a busy highway bumper-to-bumper with his fellow commuters. If there is even one fender-bender[3] along my route to work, I can be delayed up to an hour. Perhaps Blaise didn't happen to read the recent study by the National Highway Traffic Safety **Administration** which found

Self-driving cars could help prevent this.

that self-driving cars could reduce traffic congestion by more than seventy-five percent. The computers driving the cars will be able to communicate and basically choreograph[4] their own dance, moving around one another without having to slow down to a crawl. The technology would allow cars to check in with each other, anticipate[5] their movements, and work around them.

Q Why does the author think that computers make better drivers than humans do? Underline at least three things.

Computers just do some things better than people do—and more importantly, they can perform several tasks **concurrently**. They can't be distracted by birds, billboards, or loud motorcycles. They also can't drink, take drugs, or get tired. Ninety percent of all vehicular accidents are caused by the drivers' own errors. A computer, however, is far less likely to make any kind of slip-up[6] that might result from such mistakes. Once human error is taken out of the **equation**, traffic accidents—and **consequently**, deaths and injuries—plummet[7].

One of Blaise's complaints about self-driving cars was that the technology would be too expensive. He claimed that only a small percentage of the general population would be able to afford it, making any positive impacts too small to be worth the expense. But **preliminary** estimates by the non-profit group Eno Center for Transportation predict that if only ten percent of the vehicles on the road were self-driving, 1,100 lives could

---

[1] **acclaimed** *adj.* popular and respected
[2] **champion (of something)** *n.* a promoter or advocate of something
[3] **fender-bender** *n.* a minor car accident
[4] **choreograph** *v.* to design or arrange the movements of a dance

[5] **anticipate** *v.* to expect what could happen in the future and prepare for it
[6] **slip-up** *n.* a mistake
[7] **plummet** *v.* to decrease rapidly

Self-driving cars could also prevent this from happening so often.

be saved a year in the US alone. Forget about cutting my morning commute to the office down by a few minutes—this technology could actually save lives.

Like most technologies, self-driving cars will, of course, be expensive. The cost of the software, sensors, and power alone for one of these cars could well exceed $100,000 per vehicle. But Blaise's weak argument against the cost will soon become irrelevant. As with any technology, the cost will eventually go down. In the early 1970s, a personal home computer could cost tens of thousands of dollars, but today you can buy a slim, stylish laptop for only a few hundred dollars. There's no reason to assume that the cost of self-driving cars wouldn't go the same way.

As the cost of self-driving cars goes down, the benefits will only continue to increase. Once ninety percent of the cars on the road are self-driving, 4.2 billion accidents could be avoided, and 21,700 lives saved. And lives won't be the only thing being saved—when cars can **anticipate** braking and accelerating, they will use less gas, costing their owners less money and helping our ailing environment.

Do you know what else the self-driving car will save? Sanity[8]. How many poor drivers have ever cried out in frustration after their third attempt at trying to parallel park[9] their car? The technology for a self-parking car is already out there. At the 2013 International Consumer Electronics Show, the Audi RS7 Sportback SUV gave an impressive performance, parking itself neatly into a spot while the driver stood on the curb, giving the vehicle commands from a smartphone app. No scratches. No bumps. No need to leave an awkward note on someone's windshield, apologizing for the new dent you gave his or her new convertible.

(A) With over 800,000 driverless miles logged[10] (and counting), Google is presently number one. (B) That's 800,000 miles without a single crash. (C) And Google isn't holding back on where their success comes from, either. (D) Their so-called "Chauffeur system" uses lidar—basically radar and sonar combined—which can take a million measurements per second to make a 3D model of the area you're driving in. It already knows where the stationary things are—crosswalks, telephone poles, and traffic lights—and then uses lidar to fill in the gaps with moving objects. It will see the neighbor's cat dashing[11] out into the road before you do. It will know that there's a bicyclist coming up behind you. It will sense all of the things that a distracted driver might overlook, and take the actions needed to prevent any accidents. At the moment, the Chauffeur costs around $75,000, but the geniuses at Google are already working to lower the price, hopefully moving into a more affordable range by 2018.

Donald doesn't have to drive to work. Maybe he can't imagine the bliss[12] that would come from climbing into his car with the morning paper, a hot mug of coffee, and a warm croissant. He doesn't know the joy that would come from sitting back and having a relaxing, easy, accident-free commute, arriving at work feeling relaxed and without any stress or anxiety. Maybe Donald is simply uncomfortable with this new automotive **paradigm**, but I'm not—I want it!

Q What might happen if one out of ten cars on the road were self-driving? Underline the information.

C What analogy does the author use to support his prediction that self-driving cars will eventually become affordable?

Q What sensing technologies does Google's driverless car use?

---

8 **sanity** *n.* the state of positive mental health
9 **parallel park** *v.* to park parallel to a curb, between two other cars
10 **log** *v.* to travel and record a certain distance
11 **dash** *v.* to run quickly
12 **bliss** *n.* complete happiness

FOCUS ON CONTENT

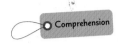

Choose the best answer.

1 What can be inferred about author Donald Blaise?
- a. He thinks that human drivers make too many errors.
- b. He knows the author of "Drive My Car . . . Please" personally.
- c. He prefers to remain in control of his own car.
- d. He does not typically write about new technology.

2 Which of the following is NOT true according to the article?
- a. Self-driving cars would result in seventy-five percent fewer traffic fatalities each year.
- b. Self-driving cars could reduce traffic congestion by over half of its current level.
- c. The computers in self-driving cars will actually communicate with those of other cars.
- d. The operating systems in self-driving vehicles can do several things at once.

3 Which of the following does the author mention as being advantages of self-driving cars? (More than one answer is possible.)
- a. Increased safety
- b. Low starting costs
- c. Higher economic output
- d. Improved the mental health of drivers
- e. Greater energy efficiency

4 Where does the following sentence fit best in paragraph 9? Choose one of the letters (A) to (D).

| Audi isn't even the leader in this technology. |

    a. (A)   b. (B)   c. (C)   d. (D)

5 Which of the following is true of lidar, according to paragraph 9?
- a. It uses cameras to locate objects near the car.
- b. Its first version will be developed by 2018.
- c. Its price has already dropped significantly.
- d. It can sense moving objects in all directions.

IDEAS IN ACTION

Talk about the questions with a partner.

1 Do you think people in your country would like self-driving cars? Explain.

2 Can you think of any drawbacks to self-driving vehicles?

CRITICAL THINKING

Identifying Circular Reasoning

Fallacies are mistaken beliefs. They are based on unsound, or bad, arguments. Fallacies are unsound in the sense that they do not follow the rules of valid arguments even though they may seem to. It's important to recognize such misleading arguments so that you aren't convinced by them.

One common fallacy is circular reasoning, or begging the question. In this kind of argument, the conclusion is included as one of the premises. When speakers or writers use circular reasoning, they assume that what they are trying to prove is true. Look at the following example:

This toy is now so popular because it is the best-selling toy on the market.
    conclusion   =   premise

To prove that the toy is popular, this argument assumes that it is popular (although the premise is restated as "it is the best-selling on the market"). Thus, the argument basically says: "This toy is popular because it is popular." Be careful not to be fooled by fallacies like this one.

❶ Read the excerpt from Reading 2 and answer the questions that follow.

I was surprised by [author Donald Blaise's] argument against this exciting new technology. How could a champion of new ideas be against self-driving cars? Though he acknowledges that their use in the future is very likely, he goes on to say: "Self-driving cars are a terrible idea because a human being has no control over the vehicle!"

    1. Find and underline an example of circular reasoning in the excerpt.
    2. Circle the conclusion and underline the premise.
    3. Circle the correct answer choice: The premise (supports / restates) the conclusion.

❷ Read the arguments below and answer the questions that follow.

Argument A: She must be telling the truth because she is definitely not lying.
    1. Circle the conclusion and underline the premise.
    2. Circle the correct answer choice: The premise (supports / restates) the conclusion.

Argument B: He must not be hungry because he said that he's just eaten a big meal.
    1. Circle the conclusion and underline the premise.
    2. Circle the correct answer choice: The premise (supports / restates) the conclusion.

Argument C: Sally is a science teacher because she teaches third-grade science.
    1. Circle the conclusion and underline the premise.
    2. Circle the correct answer choice: The premise (supports / restates) the conclusion.

VOCABULARY REVIEW

Choose the best words to fill in the blanks.

1 The country's free and open markets are a(n) _____ for other nations to follow.
   a. consequence   b. acknowledgment   c. paradigm

2 After a quick, _____ inspection, the mechanic determined that the vehicle needed a new engine.
   a. anticipated   b. administrative   c. preliminary

3 None of us _____ the public reaction to the news report and were all very surprised.
   a. acknowledged   b. anticipated   c. prepared

4 The young woman lacked the money to go to university and _____ started working after high school.
   a. concurrently   b. irrelevantly   c. consequently

5 Often when a child enters the _____, couples find that they have to make adjustments to their lives.
   a. equation   b. convertible   c. paradigm

6 Politicians often _____ the nation's problems but refuse to take responsibility for them.
   a. equate   b. acknowledge   c. anticipate

7 After graduating, the young man got a job working at the National Aeronautics and Space _____.
   a. Administration   b. Technology   c. Paradigm

8 Ms. Brown is very busy—she is managing three different projects _____.
   a. convertibly   b. eventually   c. concurrently

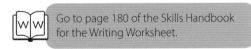

Go to page 180 of the Skills Handbook for the Writing Worksheet.

Tricks, Schemes, and Scams

How criminals fool people into giving away their money

Think About It

How can people avoid being victims of scams?

You can't cheat an honest man.

W. C. Fields

What you'll learn in this unit:		**Reading 1 / Return of the Con Artist: Tips to Protect Yourself** **Reading Skill:** Recalling and Extracting Information
		Reading 2 / Scammers Choose Their Victims Wisely **Critical Thinking Skill:** Distinguishing Generalization from Overgeneralization

Unit Project	**Make Your Point** Express your opinion about how to avoid scams

Before You Read

1 **Read the questions and circle your answers. Discuss your answers with a partner.**

1 Have you ever been tricked into giving money to someone?
   a. Yes (specify)   b. No

2 Who do you think are the most common victims of scams (tricks to get people's money)?
   a. Older people   b. Kind, trusting people
   c. Unintelligent people d. Other (specify)

3 What do you think should be done about the rise of Internet scams?
   a. People just need to be smarter and more careful, as most scams are obvious.
   b. The government should monitor and regulate the Internet more.
   c. Other (specify)

2 **Judging only by their facial expressions in these photos, which of these people do you think is the most honest and trustworthy? Discuss your choice with a partner.**

58

Reading 1

VOCABULARY PREVIEW

Read the sentence. Circle the choice that is closest to the meaning of the AWL word in bold.

1 A large church in Canada was the **target** of a criminal.
   a. a reason to feel guilty   b. something that gives help   c. object of an attack

2 There are **indications** that some types of crimes are decreasing.
   a. signs   b. results   c. rewards

3 The **unprincipled** people who commit these crimes are hard to detect.
   a. incapable   b. uneducated   c. immoral

4 **Manipulative** criminals are good at convincing their victims to do what they want.
   a. showing nervousness   b. able to control people   c. knowledgeable

5 Criminals take advantage of people's fears and **insecurities**.
   a. anger about unfairness   b. doubts about oneself   c. personal secrets

6 What can people do to protect themselves from **exploitation**?
   a. being falsely accused   b. being distrusted   c. being used unfairly

7 Instead of being emotional, try to maintain your **objectivity**.
   a. rationality   b. generosity   c. personality

8 Many criminals lie **liberally** and with ease.
   a. a lot   b. seldom   c. quickly

READING PREVIEW

This passage is an online magazine article about how criminals fool people and how to avoid being fooled.

What skills do you think criminals have that make their scams effective? Think of at least two and discuss them with a partner.

Track 9

Return of the Con Artist:
Tips to Protect Yourself

by Dr. George Simon, Ph.D.
© 2013, the author. Used by permission.

Q Why have some types of fraud increased lately?

In a poor economy, it can get pretty hard to make an honest living. That's possibly why con artists appear to be making a sort of comeback these days. Of course, they have always been around; but when times get tough, reports of people being victimized by these dishonest characters increase.

Recently, a large Christian congregation[1] in Canada was the **target** of a scam[2] in which they lost their school and day care center. And in another province, a con artist got over thirty people to pay $1,000 each toward an apartment he didn't even own. By some reports, con games are on the rise in the business world as well. In total, mortgage and land frauds[3], identity thefts, and various other tricks have cost developed economies billions over the past decade. There are some **indications** that, overall, small frauds of various types are actually on the decline, but the number of larger (and lucrative[4]) "superfrauds" has definitely increased in recent years. And while the very nature of the typical schemes and the **unprincipled** "artists" who conduct them makes them hard to detect, there are some things you can watch out for.

What is a con artist, exactly? The term *con* is short for "confidence." These **manipulative** thieves are particularly skilled in getting you to ignore any hesitancy[5] you might have, and thereby secure your confidence. As soon as they've gotten your trust, you're ready to take the inevitable fall that lies ahead. Sometimes, "running the con" takes only a few short minutes, and you only know what's happened long after the damage has already been done and the con artist is gone. Other cons take a longer time to carry out successfully. Generally speaking, the more money involved in the plan, the longer it takes to set up.

Dishonest people may use your compassion against you.

Q Underline three types of people's vulnerabilities that con artists make use of.

How do these criminals gain your trust in the first place? By preying on your greatest vulnerabilities[6]. Sometimes, those vulnerabilities are your good qualities, like your trusting nature or your compassionate[7] heart. Other times, it's your fears and **insecurities** that they take advantage of. But they can also use your character flaws, such as greed, envy, and vanity. Skilled con artists start evaluating your character from the very first moment they see you, taking note of your personality, your likes and dislikes, and especially any weakness in your ability to correctly judge the character of others.

---

[1] **congregation** *n.* a religious community

[2] **scam** *n.* a way to make money by deceiving people; *v.* to deceive in order to take others' money

[3] **fraud** *n.* a deception; a trick

[4] **lucrative** *adj.* profitable

[5] **hesitancy** *n.* reluctance; doubt

[6] **vulnerability** *n.* a weakness (vulnerable *adj.*)

[7] **compassionate** *adj.* kind; concerned about others' suffering

Is there anything you can do to protect yourself from this kind of **exploitation**? Some con artists are so skilled and charming that it's almost impossible to avoid being fooled by them. But there are some things you can do to improve the chances that you won't be a victim. First of all, you need to accept the fact that we live in an era when a lack of integrity is fairly common, so you always need to be on your guard. Never take anyone or anything at face value. And do your homework. Check things out. Verify[8]. Information is power. The more you know, the less likely you'll be taken for a ride[9]. Additionally, look for the following warning signs:

1. Beware of shallowness and smooth-talking charm. Con artists are great at using words and at making wonderful first impressions. But their charm is generally only on the surface. Their history of relationships is likely to be troubled, and it's often hard to find anyone who can assure you of their honesty. The more you find out about them, the less appealing they're likely to appear. Maintain your **objectivity**, and look for clear evidence that your interests are being respected. Talk, as they say, is cheap.

Con artists tend to be charming and make great first impressions.

2. Pay attention to any uncomfortable feelings you might have or the little voice in your head that says something just doesn't add up or sound quite right. Don't be afraid to ask questions, especially follow-up questions, even if the other person tries to make you feel overly suspicious for doing so. Many con artists lie so **liberally** and with such ease that they'll sometimes make a mistake and expose their cons accidentally. Listen very carefully, and maybe you'll get an idea of what the real agenda[10] might be.

Q Circle three pieces of advice in this paragraph.

3. Know yourself. Be aware of the kinds of things that would make you susceptible[11] to becoming a victim. Acknowledge your fears and insecurities, your deepest desires, and especially your vices[12]. Keep in mind the old saying: if something sounds too good to be true, it probably is. Often, the things that sound the sweetest to our ears are the things that either relieve our fears or appeal to our worst instincts.

Just recently, a man with a troubled past and a heroin addiction scammed another man out of $133,000 over the period of a year by claiming he needed the money to cover medical expenses for a severely ill child. The con man knew that his story wasn't really very convincing and was surprised by how easy the con was to run. But his target was a Catholic priest with a big and trusting heart, who was just too vulnerable. And although $133,000 is a lot (including all of the priest's personal savings and a large portion of his church's funds), it's hard to say what the greater crime is: the loss of all that money or a kind man's loss of faith in the basic goodness of humankind.

C What is the author's main purpose in this passage?
(1) To entertain
(2) To inform
(3) To persuade

---

[8] **verify** *v.* to make sure something is true
[9] **be taken for a ride** *idiom* to be fooled
[10] **agenda** *n.* an underlying plan or goal

[11] **susceptible** *adj.* easily influenced or affected
[12] **vice** *n.* a bad habit; a character flaw

MAPPING IDEAS

Organize the ideas from Reading 1. Review the passage and fill in the graphic organizer below.

Return of the con artist

- "Superfrauds" have
  1 _____
  lately.

- "Con" is short for
  "2 _____":
  criminals will try to gain
  your trust.

- Con artists use your
  good qualities, bad
  qualities, and your
  3 _____.

To protect yourself:
- Always be on your guard and check facts
- Be suspicious of people who are
  4 _____
- Listen and ask questions
- Be aware of your own
  5 _____

Scams cost people both their money
and their faith in humankind.

R W Before you go on, boost your reading skills. Go to page 181 of the Skills Handbook.

FOCUS ON CONTENT

1 **Circle the main idea of the passage below. For each of the other sentences, check the reason it is not the main idea.**

1 Con artists are skilled at gaining people's trust, but there are ways to avoid being a victim.
  ☐ too general   ☐ too specific   ☐ not in passage   ☐ inaccurate

2 Con artists almost always target people's good qualities, such as compassion and trust.
  ☐ too general   ☐ too specific   ☐ not in passage   ☐ inaccurate

3 It is easier to protect yourself from large frauds than from small ones.
  ☐ too general   ☐ too specific   ☐ not in passage   ☐ inaccurate

4 Large frauds have been on the rise lately because of the poor economy.
  ☐ too general   ☐ too specific   ☐ not in passage   ☐ inaccurate

2 **Mark each statement as true (T) or false (F) according to the passage.**

_____ **1** These days, small frauds seem to be increasing.

_____ **2** Frauds involving large amounts of money tend to happen over a longer period.

_____ **3** People sometimes become victims because of their own greed.

_____ **4** There is usually no need to be suspicious unless you see certain warning signs.

_____ **5** A drug addict managed to take a priest's savings and much of his church's money.

3 **Choose the best answer.**

1 What can be inferred about con artists from paragraph 4?
  a. They can guess how much money people make just by looking at them.
  b. They are skilled at identifying people's weaknesses.
  c. They usually become friends with people before trying to con them.
  d. They tend to target very self-confident people.

2 What is the main idea of paragraph 6?
  a. Despite their charm, you can often identify con artists by researching them.
  b. Con artists are generally lonely people with few friends.
  c. Con artists are skillful liars, and they are good at making people like them.
  d. You should not give people personal information until you are sure of their honesty.

THINK AND DISCUSS

 Application

1 **Read the excerpt from the reading passage.**

Return of the Con Artist: Tips to Protect Yourself

How do these criminals gain your trust in the first place? By preying on your greatest vulnerabilities. Sometimes, those vulnerabilities are your good qualities, like your trusting nature or your compassionate heart. Other times, it's your fears and insecurities that they take advantage of. But they can also use your character flaws, such as greed, envy, and vanity.

Discuss the following questions with a partner.

- Describe scams that make use of (a) people's compassion, (b) people's fears, and (c) people's greed.
- Which of the above types of scams do you think is the most effective? Why?

② **Read the following situation and write a short response.**

> Your friend saw on online ad that promises people they can make a lot of money by working at home for just a few hours a day. But, first, they have to give the company their credit card and contact information. Your friend is thinking about accepting this offer. Write an email to your friend offering advice.

_____

_____

_____

VOCABULARY REVIEW

Fill in the blanks with the correct words from the box. Change the form of the word if necessary.

objectivity	manipulative	insecurity	exploitation
liberally	target	indication	unprincipled

1 One of our co-workers is _____ and always manages to get other people to do her work.

2 Ken's _____ prevents him from asking the girl out. _____

3 Politicians are generally known for being ambitious and _____.

4 Headaches are sometimes a _____ that you are not getting enough sleep.

5 To avoid being a _____ of thieves on the subway, keep your wallet in your front pocket.

6 Of course, if you continue to spend money as _____ as you have been, you will soon be deep in debt.

7 What I especially admire about this reporter is her _____.

8 We were horrified to learn about the _____ of young children as workers in factories.

Reading 2

VOCABULARY PREVIEW

Match each AWL word in bold with its meaning from the box.

a. money spent for future profit	b. to rate
c. a person who takes part	d. to take
e. a dishonest plan	f. very sad
g. the money that a country uses	h. a limitation

_____ **1** Foreign tourists are not familiar with the local **currency**.

_____ **2** While abroad, many people don't call the police partly because of time **constraints**.

_____ **3** Older people are often tricked into making phony **investments**.

_____ **4** Many criminals' **schemes** are directed at the elderly.

_____ **5** People in the study were asked to **evaluate** how trustworthy the faces looked.

_____ **6** Those who are lonely and **depressed** are more likely to become victims.

_____ **7** Scammers **extract** money from their victims over the Internet.

_____ **8** When you fall for a scam, you are a **participant** in the crime.

READING PREVIEW

This passage is an essay about why some people are more likely to be victims of fraud than others.

What makes people more likely to be targets of scams? Think of at least two factors and discuss them with a partner.

Read the essay.

Track 10

Scammers Choose Their Victims Wisely

by Josephine Chu

I'm a frequent traveler and take pride in my ability to successfully navigate[1] unfamiliar places and cultures. That's why what happened in Shanghai was so humiliating[2]. While exploring the Nanjing Road shopping district, I was stopped by two friendly-looking young women who asked me, in English, to take their photo. I gladly did so. We chatted for a few minutes; then they said they were on their way to a tea ceremony and invited ₅ me to join them. Excited by this chance to take part in an important tradition with my two new "friends," I accepted. Imagine my shock when, after sampling teas for about half an hour, I was presented with a bill for over $100. As I learned later, I had fallen for[3] one of the most common scams in China. So while I felt like an idiot, I can take some comfort from the fact that I'm not alone; cons of all sorts are a huge industry all over the world. ₁₀ They work because some people are easier targets than others, and no one knows this better than con artists.

Q Why is the word "friends" (line 7) in quotation marks?

As my story shows, scammers know that foreign tourists make excellent victims for several reasons. If people can afford to travel abroad, they're probably pretty well-off financially with plenty of cash and credit cards in their wallets. Just as importantly, tourists are vulnerable because they're in a strange place. Chris Hagon, who heads a security consulting company, explains that "travelers are easy targets because they are unfamiliar with the environment, lack awareness, and are too trusting." As in my case, con artists might take advantage of a traveler's eagerness[4] to have a genuine encounter with a local. Or they might exploit something as simple as unfamiliarity with the **currency**. For example, while in Italy, tourists have to check their change carefully: a two-euro coin looks very much like Italy's old 500-lira coin—but the 500-lira coin is worthless. And scammers know that tourists are reluctant[5] ₂₅ to call the police because of time **constraints** and difficulty with the language.

Too many vacations are ruined by scams directed at foreign tourists. ₂₀

C Underline the appeal to authority in this paragraph.

Travelers aren't the only group that swindlers[6] have identified as targets. The elderly are also often marked as easy victims. In the US alone, people 60 and older lose almost $3 billion a year to a variety of frauds, many of which are phony[7] **investment schemes**. One might assume that this is due to a natural loss of mental sharpness as people age, but the ₃₀ true explanation isn't quite that straightforward. In a recent study at UCLA, researchers had adults of various ages look at photos of faces and **evaluate** how trustworthy they

---

[1] **navigate** *v.* to find your way around or through
[2] **humiliating** *adj.* extremely embarrassing
[3] **fall for** *phrasal v.* to be fooled by
[4] **eagerness** *n.* a feeling of strongly wanting to do something

[5] **reluctant** *adj.* hesitant; unwilling to do something
[6] **swindler** *n.* a con artist
[7] **phony** *adj.* not genuine; not real

seemed. Some of the photos showed classic signs of deception[8], such as an insincere smile. It turned out that younger adults were significantly better at identifying the potential con artists than older adults were. MRI scans showed that younger people had greater activity in the anterior insula, a part of the brain that registers danger when looking at untrustworthy faces. Apparently, people tend to start losing their ability to detect deception in their early fifties. Dr. Shelley E. Taylor, the lead author of the study, told *Science Daily*: "It's not that younger adults are better at finance or judging whether an investment is good. They're better at discerning[9] whether a person is potentially trustworthy when cues are communicated visually." In other words, the elderly are less likely to see the warning signs in a liar's face. Dr. Taylor recounted[10] how her own father was tricked into giving $6,000 to a scammer whom he described as "such a nice man."

Q At what age do people start to miss the visual signs that indicate someone is lying?

Internet con artists target emotionally vulnerable people.

So if people are young and in their home country, are they safe from con artists? Not necessarily, especially when they're online. The third category of likely scam targets is one that people all belong to at some time in their lives: the emotionally distressed[11]. A survey of 11,000 US Internet users compared the recent life experiences of those who had fallen for online scams and those who had not. Those who had been conned were more than twice as likely to have recently lost their jobs and much more likely to have experienced a financial loss in the period before the incident. Maybe most significantly, two-thirds of the victims reported feelings of isolation, compared to fewer than half of non-victims. As one of the researchers put it, "Just as a weakened immune system lowers your resistance to disease, negative life events lower your resistance to fraud." Aware of this, many con artists prey on the lonely and **depressed** by starting romantic relationships with them through Internet dating sites, and then **extracting** money from them once they've gained their trust. A study in the UK estimates that 230,000 Britons have been scammed in this way, and the number is growing rapidly.

Q Underline the main idea of this paragraph.

Being scammed feels worse than just being robbed because victims have to face the fact that they were active **participants** in the crime. Thus, the anger and stress over the financial loss is mixed with embarrassment. If, like me, you've been a victim of a scam, remember that con artists are very good at what they do. They are clever amateur[12] psychologists who know when people are most vulnerable and how to take advantage of it. Now that you have this knowledge, too, you can take steps to protect yourself. For starters, don't accept any invitations to tea ceremonies from strangers.

---

[8] **deception** *n.* trickery; lying or cheating
[9] **discern** *v.* to distinguish; to see and understand differences
[10] **recount** *v.* to tell; to narrate

[11] **distressed** *adj.* upset; in pain
[12] **amateur** *adj.* engaging in something as a pastime rather than as a profession

FOCUS ON CONTENT

1 **Choose the best answer.**

1 Which of the following best states the main idea of the passage?
   a. Con artists tend to victimize travelers, the elderly, and troubled people.
   b. Victims of scams come from all races, cultures, and economic classes.
   c. Con artists study psychology to learn how to identify and trick their victims.
   d. Scams succeed because people are all vulnerable at some point in their lives.

2 Which is NOT mentioned in paragraph 2 as a reason that con artists target tourists?
   a. Tourists usually have plenty of money.
   b. Tourists don't speak the local language.
   c. Tourists aren't used to the local currency.
   d. Tourists are afraid of the local police.

3 What can be inferred from paragraph 2?
   a. Many con artists who target tourists are not locals.
   b. People should not carry cash when traveling abroad.
   c. Some Italian con artists give tourists 500-lira coins as change.
   d. Italian police are not usually helpful to foreign tourists.

4 According to paragraph 3, younger adults are better than older adults at _____.
   a. knowing which investments will succeed
   b. knowing how to manage money in general
   c. identifying liars by how they look
   d. identifying liars by how they speak

5 According to paragraph 4, scam victims are more likely than non-victims to_____.
   a. be seriously ill
   b. feel lonely
   c. have low-paying jobs
   d. spend a lot of time online

2 **Complete the sentences with information from the passage.**

1 When in Shanghai, the author was shocked to receive _____.

2 Tourists often don't go to the police because of _____.

3 Looking at untrustworthy faces, younger adults showed more activity in

_____.

4 The US survey showed that many scam victims had recently lost _____.

IDEAS IN ACTION

Talk about the questions with a partner.

1 How can international travelers avoid becoming victims of con artists?

2 Are you good at judging whether someone is lying to you? Do you think you could identify a skilled con artist by how he or she looks and sounds?

CRITICAL THINKING

Distinguishing Generalization from Overgeneralization

Some arguments include generalizations. A **generalization** is a claim about a whole group or class of things. For example, the following are all generalizations.

- Fried foods are unhealthy.
- Americans have no interest in professional soccer.
- The best rock musicians are from the UK.

Usually, what makes a generalization convincing is examples. The more examples an argument gives, the more convincing it is. For example:

- Fried foods are unhealthy. French fries are high in fat and cholesterol. And so are potato chips, deep-fried chicken, and onion rings.

This generalization is fairly convincing because a few examples are given. However, if there are quite a few exceptions to a generalization, it is an **overgeneralization**. Overgeneralizations can be misleading and unfair, such as "Americans have no interest in professional soccer." While soccer is not among the four most popular sports in America, there are still plenty of Americans who are interested in professional soccer.

In order to avoid overgeneralizations, writers should include *qualifying* expressions. These expressions show that the statement is not or may not be true in all cases. They include *most, some, a few, several, usually, often, probably, likely,* and *may/might,* among others. For example, "Most Americans have no interest in professional soccer" is somewhat more acceptable. However, claims sound weaker when they are qualified, so many writers and speakers avoid them. As a critical thinker, you should watch out for overgeneralizations.

① Look at the generalizations from Reading 2. Underline the qualifying expressions.

1 If people can afford to travel abroad, they're probably pretty well-off financially with plenty of cash and credit cards in their wallets..

2 Apparently, people tend to start losing their ability to detect deception in their early fifties.

3 In other words, the elderly are less likely to see the warning signs in a liar's face.

2 **Rewrite the following overgeneralizations from Reading 2. Use qualifying expressions.**

1 Foreign tourists make excellent victims for several reasons.

→ _____

2 Tourists are reluctant to call the police because of time constraints and difficulty with the language.

→ _____

VOCABULARY REVIEW

Fill in the blanks with the correct words from the box. Change the form of the word if necessary.

depressed	investment	currency	constraint
extract	participant	scheme	evaluate

1 All _____ in the talent show must be in the auditorium by 7 p.m. tomorrow.

2 The UK still uses the pound as its _____; it has not adopted the euro.

3 When I feel _____, I go running; it usually makes me feel better.

4 The country's constitution places strict _____ on the power of the president.

5 About thirty percent of the world's oil is _____ from under the sea.

6 Part of a manager's job is to _____ his or her employees once a year.

7 Grandpa is retired, but he still makes money from his many _____.

8 The prisoners came up with a complex _____ to escape.

Go to page 182 of the Skills Handbook for the Writing Worksheet.

Think About It

How do you think you could improve your memory?

Memory is the diary that we all carry about with us.

Oscar Wilde

What you'll learn in this unit:		**Reading 1 / How to Maximize Your Memory** **Reading Skill:** Making Inferences
		Reading 2 / Everyday Tips for a Better Memory **Critical Thinking Skill:** Understanding Research Studies
Unit Project		**Make Your Point** Explain how to improve your memory

Before You Read

1 Have you ever tried to remember something but couldn't? Have you forgotten something that you needed to remember? Look at the examples below and circle any that you have forgotten before. Then share one example with a partner.

I forgot . . .

to do my homework

a person's name

a special date   my phone

an event

a password

a place or location

to eat

to respond to a message

2 Think of a memory that is so important to you that you will never forget it, such as a vacation, a special day, etc. Talk about it with a partner.

VOCABULARY PREVIEW

Match each AWL word with its meaning from the box.

a. the act of keeping within	b. to indicate
c. designated	d. an agreement
e. in an opposite way	f. visuals in the mind
g. similar	h. a situation

_____ **1** Some people believe the best way to improve memory **retention** is to repeat something over and over again to yourself.

_____ **2** Linking information to facts and related knowledge is the **so-called** "elaborative" processing strategy.

_____ **3** **Conversely**, the approaches that language study guides used did not do as well.

_____ **4** Improving your memory is **analogous** to increasing your muscle strength.

_____ **5** One method is to connect the information with **imagery** such as a familiar place or picture.

_____ **6** There is a **correspondence** between how good a person's memory is and how much that person practices what he or she is trying to remember.

_____ **7** This **denotes** that not many students use self-testing when they are preparing for exams.

_____ **8** In most **contexts**, saying information over and over again is not as effective for memorization as is knowing the meaning of the information.

READING PREVIEW

This passage is an article about memory improvement. The author considers different methods that people can use to become better at remembering information.

There are various methods that people use to help them remember important information. What do you do? Think of some ways and discuss them with a partner.

Track 11

How to Maximize Your Memory

by Jon Simons
© 2012, Guardian News and Media, Ltd. Used by permission.

If you're studying for an exam, learning a new language, or just interested in maximizing your memory for everyday life, here are some strategies that might help.

Rehearsal[1]

The brain is often compared to a muscle, the suggestion being that if you exercise the brain, its function will improve. **Analogous** to a bodybuilder strengthening his arms by [5] lifting weights, you too can improve your memory by repeating over and over to yourself the information you wish to remember.

For years, researchers considered that "rehearsing" information in this way was required for memory **retention**. This view fits with the instinct[2] to repeat to ourselves something that we want to remember, like a phone number, in the hope that it "sticks." There is [10] evidence that the more an item is rehearsed, the greater the possibility of long-term retention. In one study, participants were given a list of words and told to rehearse the list out loud, and then asked to recall[3] the words. There was a **correspondence** between their memory retrieval[4] and the amount of rehearsal that was done. But, in almost all **contexts**, rehearsal proved to be much less effective than strategies that involve thinking [15] about the meaning of the information to be remembered.

"Elaborative" Processing

Many people imagine that actors memorize their lines by using rote[5] rehearsal, but research suggests that this is not always the case. Psychiatrists have found that some actors learn their lines by focusing on the core meanings of words as opposed to the [20] words themselves. They also concentrate on the motivations of the character that they will be portraying. This **so-called** "elaborative"[6] processing strategy involves relating the information to associated facts and relevant knowledge.

In one study, participants learned sentences either by simply studying them (e.g., "The man was angry at his boss.") or by making an elaborate continuation[7] to the sentence [25] (e.g., "The man was angry at his boss because he had to work on weekends."). The elaboration method improved memory for the sentence significantly. This suggests that the cognitive[8] effort involved led to deeper encoding[9] of the original sentence.

Another experiment compared different kinds of elaboration to see which might be most useful when studying for exams. One group of participants was given topics in the form of questions to think about before reading a text. A second group was asked to just study the text. The researchers found that reviewing the text with relevant questions in mind improved retention and recall of the material.

 [30]

Research shows that students have an easier time remembering information if it has meaning to them. [35]

Margin note:
C What claim does the author make about how people remember phone numbers?

Footnotes:
[1] **rehearsal** n. a practice to improve some activity in preparation for a performance
[2] **instinct** n. natural behavior that is not learned
[3] **recall** v. to remember something; n. the ability to remember something
[4] **retrieval** n. the act of getting something back; recovery
[5] **rote** n. a method that relies on routine and repetition rather than deep understanding
[6] **elaborative** adj. related to adding detail
[7] **continuation** n. the act or state of causing something to keep happening
[8] **cognitive** adj. related to the activities of the mind
[9] **encode** v. to convert information so that it can be received by the brain

Mnemonics[10]

A visit to any bookshop will reveal shelves of self-help books about using mnemonics for improving memory. The method of loci is perhaps the most well-known mnemonic technique. It involves thinking of **imagery** that links information with familiar locations. For instance, when trying to remember a list of words, you might visualize walking between the rooms in your home. In each room, you remember a word by forming an image that combines the word with a feature of the room. If given the word "apple," you might imagine a painting of an apple in your living room. Then, you will be able to retrieve the list of words by mentally walking through the rooms of your house again. One study found that people using the loci method could recall more than ninety percent of a list of fifty words after studying them just once.

Some of the world's most successful memory geniuses use mnemonic strategies. Dominic O'Brien, British author and eight-time winner of the World Memory Championships, spent twelve hours at a restaurant in London going through fifty-four packs of randomly ordered playing cards. He looked at each card once and then managed to recall 2,800 of the 2,808 cards in the correct order, an amazing level of success.

Techniques such as loci can be adapted to help you remember day-to-day information like appointments, birthdays, chores, tasks, and so on. The key with mnemonics is creating the most interesting visual images possible. The more creative and elaborative you can be, the greater the chance of success.

Q Why does the author mention Dominic O'Brien?

Retrieval Practice

Evidence suggests that repeatedly testing yourself on the information you have learned can greatly enhance retention. In a number of experiments, participants learned lists of words in three conditions: standard (study, test, study, test); repeated study (study, study, study, test); and repeated test (study, test, test, test). The repeated study group had three times as much exposure to the words as the repeated test group. If learning occurs only when studying, then they should have had better memory, but comparable immediate learning was found in each of the experiments. Meanwhile, if retention is measured after a one-week delay, repeated retrieval testing can lead to noticeably better recall than repeated studying. This is true even if the studying involves an elaborative learning strategy.

The importance of testing memory has been shown to apply to a number of everyday learning situations. Take learning foreign languages as an example. Experts have found that repeated testing during the learning period resulted in eighty percent accurate vocabulary recall when examined a week later. **Conversely**, strategies used in language study guides saw success rates drop to thirty percent. What is more interesting is that when the participants were asked to predict their later performance, they said they didn't think that the repeated testing method appeared to give them any advantage.

Q What technique do experts say is the most effective way to learn a foreign language?

This impression **denotes** that students rarely use self-testing strategies when studying for exams, and other research supports this. When students do self-test, it is often to assess what they have learned, rather than to enhance their long-term retention of the material. Perhaps the fact that repeated study feels less demanding than repeatedly testing leads people to prefer the first approach. But the evidence suggests that active approaches to learning such as repeated retrieval practice can yield[11] greater dividends[12].

---

[10] **mnemonic** *n*. a process, system, or technique that helps with improving memory

[11] **yield** *v*. to produce

[12] **dividend** *n*. anything received as a reward or bonus

MAPPING IDEAS

Organize the ideas from Reading 1. Review the passage and fill in the graphic organizer below.

Techniques for _____

Rehearsal

- Ex.: The more people [2] _____ by repeating the things they want to remember, the better they will be at [3] _____ them.

[4] _____

- Ex.: Actors [5] _____ their lines by focusing on the [6] _____ of words or their character's motivations.

Mnemonics

- Ex.: Matching a word with [7] _____, like picturing the word as [8] _____ in a house, is a very effective memory technique.

[9] _____

- Ex.: Students who do [10] _____ are better at [11] _____ that they are studying.

> R W Before you go on, boost your reading skills. Go to page 183 of the Skills Handbook.

FOCUS ON CONTENT

1 **Circle the main idea of the passage below. For each of the other sentences, check the reason it is not the main idea.**

1 Memory techniques help a person remember things more easily.

☐ too general   ☐ too specific   ☐ not in passage   ☐ inaccurate

2 Mnemonics is the least effective memory improvement system.

☐ too general   ☐ too specific   ☐ not in passage   ☐ inaccurate

3 There are several methods that can increase a person's memory.

☐ too general   ☐ too specific   ☐ not in passage   ☐ inaccurate

4 The tools that teachers use to help students prepare for tests can improve memory.

☐ too general   ☐ too specific   ☐ not in passage   ☐ inaccurate

② Choose the best answer.

1 Which of the following statements is true according to the passage?

    a. Not many people know the method of loci because it is a new technique.

    b. Most students prefer to do repeated testing as opposed to repeated study.

    c. Studies show that memory techniques can only be learned at a young age.

    d. Elaborative processing is more effective than rehearsal for memory recall.

2 What is Dominic O'Brien famous for?

    a. He is the inventor of an effective memory technique.

    b. He has performed incredible feats of memorization.

    c. He has written books about how to win at card games.

    d. He is the creator of a world-class memory competition.

3 Before the study, what were the participants' attitude to the repeated testing method?

    a. They knew that it would help them score higher on the final exam.

    b. They thought it would take too much time.

    c. They did not see how it would be any better than the other strategies.

    d. They were excited to learn a new memory technique.

4 What activity did the author compare the rehearsal technique to?

    a. Lifting weights

    b. Learning foreign languages

    c. Studying for a test

    d. Building a home

THINK AND DISCUSS

① Read the excerpt from the reading passage.

How to Maximize Your Memory

If you're studying for an exam, learning a new language, or just interested in maximizing your memory for everyday life, here are some strategies that might help.

Discuss the following question with a partner.

- The ways that people remember information are important, but so too are the reasons for needing to remember. For example, students need to remember information in order to pass a test. What are some other situations in which it is important for a person to have a good memory?

② The method of loci uses imagery, such as a symbol or a mental picture, to recall memories. People can also be reminded of a memory by their senses, such as a taste, smell, or sound. What image or sensory experience causes you to recall a memory? Write a short paragraph describing the image or sense and the memory.

_____

_____

_____

_____

_____

_____

VOCABULARY REVIEW

Fill in the blanks with the correct words from the box. Change the form of the word if necessary.

analogous	imagery	retention	conversely
denote	correspondence	context	so-called

1 His analysis shows a close _____ between the two sets of data.

2 Football is _____ to a chess game because both require strategy to win.

3 The "Wi-Fi" sign _____ that this area is a wireless Internet hotspot.

4 Fluid _____ in the lungs can cause breathing difficulty.

5 In the social and cultural _____ of the 1800s, it would have been considered strange for a woman to wear pants.

6 He enjoys going out to eat at restaurants often; _____, she prefers to cook and eat at home.

7 The _____ snow leopard gets its name from the snow habitat it lives in.

8 This painting is famous for its colorful _____, particularly the bright flowers and the sunset.

VOCABULARY PREVIEW

Read the sentence. Circle the choice that is closest to the meaning of the AWL word in bold.

1 Scientists have found proof that **documents** how people can improve their memory.
   a. details   b. hides   c. delivers

2 A medical **journal** reported that healthy children have better memories than unhealthy children.
   a. product advertisement   b. research paper   c. specialized magazine

3 A medical organization **endorses** certain kinds of video games as a way to improve memory.
   a. hinders   b. promotes   c. persuades

4 While sleeping, people's brains **channel** short-term memories to other parts of the brain to turn them into long-term memories.
   a. chase   b. direct   c. squeeze

5 Normal aging causes brains to **decline** in size, but exercise can slow down this process.
   a. advance   b. reshape   c. lessen

6 Students often try to **retain** as much information as they can by memorizing everything just before a test.
   a. keep in memory   b. quickly absorb   c. totally disregard

7 There are serious mental conditions that **induce** severe memory loss.
   a. cause   b. prevent   c. inspire

8 Aerobic activity plays an important role in the **enhancement** of memory.
   a. support   b. prevention   c. improvement

READING PREVIEW

This passage talks about steps that people can take to improve their memory. The author explains how a healthy mind and body can help people be less forgetful.

- Discuss with a partner. What can people do to stay healthy?
- Discuss with a partner. What can people do to stay healthy? How do you think healthy habits and activities could help improve memory?

79

Everyday Tips for a Better Memory

by Jon Maes / Language Cradle Consulting

Have you every wished that you could remember something that you had forgotten? Perhaps it was a story you wanted to tell someone. Maybe you had trouble recalling information such as a person's name or a phone number. Perhaps you had forgotten an important date such as a family member's or a friend's birthday. The truth is you are not alone. Everyone deals with these sorts of memory difficulties at one time or another in life. 5

However, what if there are ways to improve your memory and enhance your brainpower so you have a greater capacity to store and recall details? While science has not solved the entire puzzle of human memory, it has certainly made great strides[1]. With convincing evidence that **documents** their findings, researchers are able to propose effective ways 10 of improving people's memory retention and recollection[2].

People lose their memory with age, but researchers are working to find ways of slowing down this process.

Q What did the American Academy of Neurology study conclude? Underline the information.

To begin with, there are a number of physical considerations for preventing memory loss. The first is being mindful of how much you eat. A study by the American Academy of Neurology concluded that overeating is likely to increase a 15 person's chances of memory loss. Observing three groups of elderly subjects (aged 70–79) with different eating habits, it found that the group who ate the most calories above the recommended daily intake[3] had a fifty-percent greater risk of developing mild cognitive impairment[4]. This is the stage 20 between normal age-related forgetfulness and serious mental ailments[5] that **induce** substantial[6] memory loss, such as Alzheimer's disease.

Q What effect does eating fish produce on the hippocampus?

Similarly, certain foods can actually help prevent memory loss as well as retention and recollection. Some foods have even been nicknamed "brain food" because tests show that they have nutrients that improve people's mental functions. A good example is fish 25 that are high in a fatty acid called omega 3. Researchers have found that omega 3 from eating fish—or taking fish oil supplements[7]—accumulates in the hippocampus, an area in the central part of the brain where many key memory functions take place. Omega 3 improves communication between memory cells there. A more productive hippocampus leads to better retention and recollection of memories. 30

Getting a good night's sleep is also known to consolidate[8] and strengthen memories. This is because memory capabilities are linked to both the quantity and quality of sleep.

---

[1] **stride** *n.* a forward leap; progress
[2] **recollection** *n.* the act of remembering
[3] **intake** *n.* the amount of something that is taken in, such as by eating or drinking
[4] **impairment** *n.* the state or condition of being lesser in strength or ability

[5] **ailment** *n.* a sickness, illness, or disorder
[6] **substantial** *adj.* significant; great
[7] **supplement** *n.* a product that people ingest for added nutrition
[8] **consolidate** *v.* to join together into a whole; to combine

Doctors recommend sleeping a minimum of six hours a day, with eight hours being ideal. During sleep—specifically in the later stages—the brain works to restore its memory functions. It also uses this time to **channel** short-term memories to other areas of the brain by making connections so that the memories become more permanent. This consolidation process leads to what is called long-term memory, which allows people to remember experiences that happened the day before, weeks or months earlier, and even years in the past.

No discussion of memory **enhancement** would be complete without talking about the importance of regular aerobic exercise. Experts believe that exercise can make the hippocampus grow, which enhances its functioning. A study published in the **journal** *Brain Research* indicates that physically fit children have a twelve-percent larger hippocampus. These children also performed better on memory tests than children who did not get as much exercise. Also, research shows that adults who walked for forty minutes three days a week over the course of a year displayed a hippocampus growth rate of two percent. While two percent may not seem like much, it should appear more significant when compared to the annual one percent **decline** in size from normal aging in people who do not get enough physical activity.

Q What evidence is used to show that children who exercise have better memory abilities?

Besides eating carefully, sleeping enough, and getting enough exercise, there are other steps people can take to improve their memory. An area of particular interest to students is their study habits. One practice that should be avoided is cramming[9]. This is the habit of trying to **retain** a considerable amount of information in a short period of time, such as the night before a test. Scientists have found that people remember information longer if their study sessions are spaced out over a week or more. Another effective strategy is to use retrieval methods, such as doing self-tests, between study sessions instead of merely memorizing the material. Studies have shown that students who use these techniques remember fifty percent more of the material they are studying.

Believe it or not, computer and video games can stimulate memory enhancement. In Sweden, research using game therapy on patients with serious brain injuries found that their memory abilities improved significantly in as little as five weeks. The American Psychological Association has even **endorsed** certain types of video games—especially those that involve solving puzzles or role-playing—for their memory enhancement abilities.

All things considered, there is no "magic pill" for memory enhancement. It takes a concerted[10] effort to make important lifestyle changes and a commitment to strategies that work to improve one's memory. So, how about it? Don't you want to protect and enhance your memory?

Q What does the author mean by saying there is no "magic pill" for improving memory?

[9] **cram** *v.* to study hard at the last minute for a test

[10] **concerted** *adj.* done with great intensity or determination

FOCUS ON CONTENT

1   **Choose the best answer.**

1   What is the passage mainly about?
    a.   Various kinds of memory difficulties
    b.   Different methods for improving one's memory
    c.   Physical problems that cause memory loss
    d.   The reason that gaming can enhance memory

2   What is the author's opinion about cramming?
    a.   It is an effective way to study for a test.
    b.   Schools should prohibit students from doing it.
    c.   It has no effect on a person's memory.
    d.   Some other study methods are more effective.

3   How does exercise improve a person's memory?
    a.   It raises a person's heart rate, forcing more blood into the brain.
    b.   It causes the hippocampus to grow larger, which increases its functionality.
    c.   It releases chemicals that make people happier, which in turn helps the brain.
    d.   It extends people's lives, so more memories are generated.

4   Which of the following can be inferred from the passage about Alzheimer's disease?
    a.   It is a mental condition that only very old people have.
    b.   People who eat fewer calories are less likely to get it.
    c.   Omega 3 is known to cure the disease.
    d.   A very small percentage of people lose their memory completely.

5   How much does the hippocampus lose in size each year from normal aging?
    a.   1%   b.   2%   c.   4%   d.   12%

2   **Mark each statement as true (T) or false (F) according to the passage.**

_____ **1**   The brain is active during sleep to transfer memories to other areas of the brain.

_____ **2**   Eating fish is the only way to get omega 3.

_____ **3**   The author says that good study habits are more important than healthy eating.

_____ **4**   Walking for forty minutes three times a week can improve memory.

IDEAS IN ACTION

Talk about the questions with a partner.

1 Of the various methods that the author discusses for improving memory, which one would be easiest for you to do and which one would be hardest? Why?

2 How do the methods you mentioned in question 1 affect your memory?

CRITICAL THINKING

Understanding Research Studies

Arguments, especially those in scholarly writing, commonly refer to research studies. As with any argument, it is important to be careful with this kind of information. Most problems with research studies relate to how data is gathered.

(1) A typical study is set up to test an idea, called a **hypothesis**. For example, a researcher might want to find out if exercising enhances memory functioning.

(2) A good study needs to look at a group, but most groups are too large to look at every single individual; instead, a **sample** is selected. This sample needs to be as large as possible, and it should be representative. That is, it should include the right kinds of people and in the right proportions so that the results can be applied to the whole group.

(3) A study may want to look at one particular factor and what happens over a period of time when the factor is changed. But obviously other factors may have an effect, too. Researchers should keep as many factors the same as possible; these are called **controls**. For example, in the study about exercise and memory functioning, researchers would have to control diet, sleep, stress, and other related factors.

(4) A well-designed study should also include a **control group** in the sample, and this group is not influenced by the particular factor being tested. For instance, to be reliable, our study should have a group of people who do not exercise for the duration of the study. Then, the two groups can be compared.

① Read the excerpts from Reading 2 and answer the questions that follow.

A study by the American Academy of Neurology concluded that overeating is likely to increase a person's chances of memory loss. Observing three groups of elderly subjects (aged 70–79) with different eating habits, it found that the group who ate the most calories above the recommended daily intake had a fifty-percent greater risk of developing mild cognitive impairment.

a. Whatisthehypothesisbeingtested?_____

b. What is the sample? _____

c. Is the sample representative of the group? Explain. _____

d. Did the study include a control group? If not, explain how it could have included one. _____

_____

A study published in the journal *Brain Research* indicates that physically fit children have a twelve-percent larger hippocampus. These children also performed better on memory tests than children who did not get as much exercise.

a. What is the hypothesis being tested? _____

b. What is the sample? _____

c. Is the sample representative of the group? Explain. _____

d. Did the study include a control group? If not, explain how it could have included one. _____

_____

2 Write a short explanation about how you might design a research study to test the relationship between eating fast food and memory performance in teenagers. Include these details: hypothesis, sample, control group, procedure, and duration of study.

_____

_____

VOCABULARY REVIEW

1 Match each word to its definition.

1	retain (v.)	**a**	to bring about or cause
2	decline (v.)	**b**	the act of improving or increasing something's value, quality, etc.
3	document (v.)	**c**	to keep something, particularly in memory
4	induce (v.)	**d**	to keep careful records of an event
5	channel (v.)	**e**	a publication that deals with a particular subject or group
6	enhancement (n.)	**f**	to lead toward or in a certain direction
7	endorse (v.)	**g**	to support or actively encourage
8	journal (n.)	**h**	to drop or go down

2 Fill in the blanks with the correct words from above. Change the form of the word if necessary.

1 Some card players are able to "count cards," which involves _____ in memory details of the cards that have been played.

2 Our research paper will be published in the department's annual _____.

3 The _____ in sales lowered the company's profit for the year.

4 Researchers are trying to _____ the languages of native people in the area so there is some record of them.

5 The mayor has worked hard to _____ education and social welfare.

[w w] Go to page 184 of the Skills Handbook for the Writing Worksheet.

UNIT

7 Practice Makes Perfect

What it takes to be an expert

Think About It

What does it take to become great at something?

An expert is a man who has made all the mistakes which can be made, in a narrow field.

Niels Bohr

Reading 1 / Are Malcolm Gladwell's 10,000 Hours of Practice Really All You Need?
Reading Skill: Identifying Causes and Effects

Reading 2 / The Truth About Talent: Can Genius Be Learned or Is It Preordained?
Critical Thinking Skill: Identifying Causation and Correlation

Unit Project | **Make Your Point**
Express your ideas about what is necessary to become great at something

Before You Read

1 **Answer the questions. Discuss your answers with a partner.**

1 Think of someone famous who is extremely talented. Write his or her name. _____

2 What is he or she an expert at? _____

3 What do you know about this person? How do you think he or she became an expert?

_____

2 **Which of the following factors do you think is most important in becoming an expert at something? Rank them from most important (1) to least important (6). Discuss your choices with a partner.**

___ Natural ability

___ Amount of practice

___ Coach or teacher

___ Motivation

___ Supportive family

___ Money

Reading 1

VOCABULARY PREVIEW

Read the sentence. Circle the choice that is closest to the meaning of the AWL word in bold.

1 The debate about how someone becomes an expert is still **unresolved**.

   a. not decided   b. not important   c. not clear

2 Researchers found a wide **variability** in the number of hours that experts practiced.

   a. shift   b. measurement   c. difference

3 For expert musicians, the amount of practice **ranged** from 10,000 to 30,000 hours.

   a. started   b. increased   c. varied

4 This study **invalidates** the rule that people need 10,000 hours to master a skill.

   a. disproves   b. questions   c. responds to

5 The study mixes **data** about highly skilled experts with less skilled people.

   a. research   b. information   c. opinions

6 Another problem is Ericsson's **reliance** on just a few highly skilled performers.

   a. dependence   b. belief   c. research

7 There isn't enough information to make any conclusions **statistically**.

   a. mathematically   b. practically   c. definitely

8 Critics think Ericsson's statement is a **reversal** from a strong position to a weaker one.

   a. difference   b. turnaround   c. transformation

READING PREVIEW

This article talks about the responses of researchers to the idea of Malcolm Gladwell that it takes 10,000 hours of practice for someone to become an expert.

> Can you think of any criticisms of Malcolm Gladwell's idea? Talk about your ideas with a partner.

Track 13

Are Malcolm Gladwell's 10,000 Hours of Practice Really All You Need?

by Dan Vergano

Keep practicing, and you might become an expert. Or maybe you won't. Who knows? Not the experts, suggests an intense debate that remains **unresolved**. Made famous by *Outliers: The Story of Success*, by Malcolm Gladwell, the 2008 book's "10,000-hour rule"—the number of hours of practice needed to acquire[1] mastery of a skill—seems to be increasingly under attack. 5

"No one disputes[2] that practice is important," says psychologist David Zachary Hambrick of Michigan State University in East Lansing. "Through practice, people get better. The question is whether that is all there is to it."

Some people need to practice much more than others do in order to become a chess grand master.

Starting the debate, a study published in May 2013 in the journal *Intelligence* by Hambrick and colleagues suggested that 10 practice explains only about a third of master-level success. Hambrick's team looked at case studies of master musicians and chess players. After quizzing the players on their lifetime hours of deliberate practice (as opposed to performances or play), they concluded that practice accounted for only thirty percent 15 of success in music and thirty-four percent in chess. They also found wide **variability** in the hours of practice. Chess grand masters had put in from 832 to 24,284 hours of work, although the average was around 10,530 hours. Musicians' efforts **ranged** from 10,000 to 30,000 hours. This variability in hours of practice 20 **invalidates** the 10,000-hour rule, Hambrick suggests.

In response, psychologist K. Anders Ericsson of Florida State University in Tallahassee says that this kind of criticism inappropriately mixes **data** about less skilled folks into the analysis. Hambrick responds that Ericsson's **reliance** on only a few elite performers for his studies of expertise turns the studies into anecdotes[3]. "If we don't have enough data 25 points in the study to say anything **statistically**, then it isn't science."

In the background of the 10,000-hour rule argument are two influential, but discredited[4], scientists. The first, Francis Galton, the 19th-century father of eugenics[5], argued that heredity[6] essentially explained all talent and expertise. Galton's racist ideas inspired the Nazis' terrible notions of racial purity. The second, John Watson, the early 20th-century 30 father of behaviorism[7], argued, "Give me a dozen healthy infants, well-formed, and my own specified world to bring them up in and I'll guarantee to take any one at random

Q What do the results of Hambrick's study indicate? Underline the information.

---

[1] **acquire** *v.* to learn or develop (a skill, habit, or quality)

[2] **dispute** *v.* to argue about; to disagree

[3] **anecdote** *n.* a story, often one that is considered unreliable

[4] **discredited** *adj.* shown to be false or unreliable

[5] **eugenics** *n.* the science of improving human beings through controlled breeding

[6] **heredity** *n.* the passing down of characteristics in the genes from one generation to the next

[7] **behaviorism** *n.* the theory that behavior can be changed using rewards and punishments

and train him to become any type of specialist I might select—doctor, lawyer, artist, merchant-chief, and, yes, even beggar-man and thief, regardless of his talents, [habits],
35 tendencies, abilities, vocations, and race of his ancestors."

Today's 10,000-hour rule debate is often described as a fight over which of these extremes, nature or nurture, is more important when it comes to acquiring expertise. And the participants in the debate often paint their opponents as taking an extreme view of how expertise is acquired. Gladwell, for example, said that Ericsson is guilty of
40 "expanding and stretching" the 10,000-hour rule toward being an absolute, far from his own view of it as more of a principle for people with aptitude[8] for a skill. Ericsson notes that Gladwell's book mistakes the average of 10,000 hours that experts took to master a skill, as described in his research, for a narrow and strict requirement for all experts, established or aspiring. Aside from obvious genes for height or body size that
45 help people in sports such as basketball, Ericsson says his real position is simply that he doesn't see evidence for genes that help people acquire expert levels of performance.

"The genes might well be there; but until we definitely identify them, I think we can't go beyond that," Ericsson says. In the era of the human genome[9], he argues against a rush toward genetic explanations for things.

50 Hambrick and other 10,000-hour critics see this as "moving the goalposts" in a scientific debate, a **reversal** from an earlier strong position to a weaker one while refusing to concede[10].

Plenty of studies suggest that, aside from practice hours, individual differences help explain success, Georgia Tech's Phillip Ackerman says in *Intelligence*. Such differences
55 range from socioeconomics[11] to coaching to IQ. A *Psychology of Sport and Exercise* journal study from March 2014, for example, found no difference between the number of hours practiced by kids who grew up to be professional soccer players and the number practiced by kids who did not. The big difference between them was the amount of good coaching they received at a young age.

60 The participants in the disagreement often voice two opposing concerns. One fear Ericsson expresses is that if talent is viewed as somehow innate[12] and not the result of practice, disadvantaged kids will be cut off from opportunities in education and sports.

"Nobody is going to be able to fly," Ericsson says. "But some kids are going to be blown away by the number of things they can do if they're given the chance."

65 On the other hand, Ackerman worries that telling people they just need to practice more might set them up for failure: "The odds are pretty good, but not impossible, that if you have an IQ of 70, you're probably not going to get a Ph.D. in particle physics."

Practice, then, is just one more ingredient in success. "There aren't innate abilities. Aside from our reflexes, everything is learned in one way or the other," Ackerman says.
70 "Motivation, timing, and luck are all in there, too."

---

8   **aptitude** *n.* a natural ability to do something

9   **genome** *n.* the complete set of genes in an organism

10   **concede** *v.* to give in; to admit that something is true after first saying it is not

11   **socioeconomic** *adj.* of or relating to one's income and position in society

12   **innate** *adj.* natural; occurring from birth

Q Who are the two figures behind the debate? They are:
(1) _____, who said _____ explains all talent
(2) _____, who said anyone can be _____ to be any kind of specialist

Q What is Ericsson's actual position? Underline it.

Q What are the two opposing concerns mentioned in the reading? Underline them.

C What is this author's point of view on the topic?
(1) Biased
(2) Balanced/Impartial

MAPPING IDEAS

Organize the ideas from Reading 1. Review the passage and fill in the graphic organizer below.

The 10,000-hour rule for mastering a skill

Opponents		
Hambrick	*Galton*	*Ackerman*
• Practice only explains about a third of expertise among ¹ _____ • There is a lot of ² _____ in the amount of practice needed • Studies must look at people other than experts	• Father of ³ _____ • Heredity explains all talent and expertise	• Many other factors besides practice help explain success

Supporters		
Ericsson	*Watson*	*Gladwell*
• It's wrong to include data about less skilled people in studies • We should not assume there is a ⁴ _____ explanation; there is no evidence	• Father of ⁵ _____ • Anyone can learn any skill with enough practice	• "10,000 hours" is only a principle for people with a natural ⁶ _____ in a given field

 Before you go on, boost your reading skills. Go to page 185 of the Skills Handbook.

FOCUS ON CONTENT

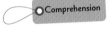

1   **Circle the main idea of the passage. For each of the other sentences, check the reason it is not the main idea.**

   1   There is no agreement among experts about whether practice alone can lead to expertise.
   ☐ too general   ☐ too specific   ☐ not in passage   ☐ inaccurate

   2   Malcolm Gladwell's view has been misrepresented as an extreme position.
   ☐ too general   ☐ too specific   ☐ not in passage   ☐ inaccurate

   3   There is strong evidence for a genetic explanation of talent.
   ☐ too general   ☐ too specific   ☐ not in passage   ☐ inaccurate

   4   Malcolm Gladwell's ideas about practice have sparked debate among experts.
   ☐ too general   ☐ too specific   ☐ not in passage   ☐ inaccurate

1 Why did Hambrick include data about less skilled people in his study?

    a. Because there are too few experts to conduct research on

    b. Because not enough research is done on this group of people

    c. Because more data is necessary in order to make the findings meaningful

    d. Because all good research studies require a control group

2 According to paragraph 6, in what way did Ericsson misrepresent Gladwell's views?

    a. He made Gladwell's position seem like a rule, which is too extreme.

    b. He said that Gladwell's views were the same as Galton's.

    c. He said that Gladwell's view is a principle for certain highly skilled people.

    d. He interpreted Gladwell's views to be very different from his own.

3 Which factor did Ackerman say was the most significant for kids that grew up to be professional soccer players?

    a. Their socioeconomic background

    b. The amount of natural ability they displayed

    c. The number of hours they had spent practicing

    d. The quality of their instruction at an early stage

4 According to Ackerman, what danger is implicit in the view that expertise only requires more practice?

    a. It could mean that some disadvantaged children will not have opportunities.

    b. It puts too much pressure on children to perform at their peak.

    c. It might mean future disappointment and frustration for some children.

    d. It puts certain children with lower IQs at a disadvantage.

THINK AND DISCUSS

① **Read the excerpt from the reading passage.**

Are Malcolm Gladwell's 10,000 Hours of Practice Really All You Need?

Practice, then, is just one more ingredient in success. "There aren't innate abilities. Aside from our reflexes, everything is learned in one way or the other," Ackerman says. "Motivation, timing, and luck are all in there, too."

Discuss the following question with a partner.

- Choose one field, such as sports, music, mathematics, etc. What might these factors—innate ability, motivation, timing, and luck—mean for someone who wants to be an expert in that field?

② **What would you say to someone who feels like he or she doesn't have any talent for doing something? Write a brief response.**

_____

_____

_____

_____

_____

VOCABULARY REVIEW

Fill in the blanks with the correct words from the box. Change the form of the word if necessary.

data	invalidate	range	reliance
reversal	statistically	unresolved	variability

1 There are many exceptions, so do not put too much _____ on these rules for classification.

2 Not all adult hummingbirds are the same size; in fact, there is a lot of _____ in their sizes.

3 The trend is interesting, but it can't be confirmed _____ without analyzing relevant figures.

4 The group's activities are varied, _____ from community clean-up projects to fundraisers.

5 The analysis is based on _____ collected over a three-year period.

6 Unfortunately, the legal issues surrounding this technology remain _____.

7 If a liar says lying is wrong, he might be a hypocrite, but it does not _____ his statement.

8 Public outrage led to a hasty _____ of the policy only a month after the government implemented it.

VOCABULARY PREVIEW

Match each AWL word in bold with its meaning from the box.

a. to say something is untrue	b. a part of
c. to direct toward	d. to last
e. to suggest	f. to calculate
g. to guess something based on evidence	h. early

_____ **1** One might **infer** that an extremely talented person must have been born with skills beyond the average.

_____ **2** There are **initial** differences in ability between talented children and others.

_____ **3** These differences do not **persist** through years of practice.

_____ **4** We assume people are talented because we only see a small **proportion** of the practice they do.

_____ **5** This **implies** that everyone could become incredibly talented if they have enough practice.

_____ **6** Can someone who failed math ever **compute** difficult math problems?

_____ **7** In saying this, we do not **deny** the ideas of Darwin.

_____ **8** We can **orient** children to a better way of thinking by focusing on their effort instead of on their ability.

READING PREVIEW

This article is about how the way talent is understood can affect attitudes toward improvement.

How do you think the following ideas might affect children?

- Talent comes from practice.
- Talent is something people are born with.

Track 14

The Truth About Talent:
Can Genius Be Learned or Is It Preordained?

by Matthew Syed
© 2011, The Independent. Used by permission.

Darwin's idea that individuals fail or flourish[1] by virtue of inherited characteristics has been a triumph[2]. But Darwinism has transformed into a rather different idea: the idea that prowess[3] depends, in large part, on the right genetic inheritance. *Talent* is the word society uses to rationalise this idea, the notion that brilliant mathematicians, scientists, sportsmen, and musicians are born with excellence encoded in their DNA. People **infer** 5 that these experts must have been blessed with skills way beyond the norm. But what if this tempting idea is all wrong?

After all, what is talent? Some people certainly think they know it when they see it. As the director of a violin school put it: "Talent is something a top coach can spot in young musicians that marks them out as destined for greatness." But how does the director 10 know that a performer who seems quite gifted hasn't had many hours of special training? How does he know that the **initial** differences in ability between this youngster and the rest will **persist** through years of practice?

In fact, he doesn't, as many studies have demonstrated. A ground-breaking investigation of British musicians, for example, found that the top performers had learned no faster 15 than those who reached lower levels. Hour after hour, the various groups improved at almost identical rates. The difference was simply that top performers had practiced for more hours.

Precisely the same insight is revealed by looking at child prodigies—boys and girls who reach world-class levels of performance in their teens or even earlier. At first sight, 20 they seem to have been blessed with amazing skills. But a closer inspection reveals a very different story. Math prodigy Rudiger Gamm, for instance, was once described as a "walking miracle" by one science magazine. But now consider that Gamm practices for at least four hours every day. His excellence is not hardwired[4]—it emerged through practice.

The illusion of talent arises because outside observers only see a tiny **proportion** of the work that goes into the construction of virtuosity[5]. If these observers were to examine the many hours of practice by world-class performers, the skills would not seem quite so mystical[6] or so inborn[7].

 25

So, does this **imply** that "ordinary" people could perform amazing feats[8] with sufficient practice? Could those who failed math really **compute** multi-digit calculations like Gamm? In 1896, Alfred Binet, a French psychologist, performed an experiment to find

Many think that genius arises 30 from talent because society often underestimates the amount of effort that goes into improving ability.

C What is the main point of the article? Underline it.

Q What was the finding of the study of British musicians?

---

[1] **flourish** *v.* to develop in a very healthy or strong way
[2] **triumph** *n.* a great victory or achievement
[3] **prowess** *n.* a high degree of skill in a particular area or field
[4] **hardwired** *adj.* determined by genetics

[5] **virtuosity** *n.* great skill, particularly in the arts
[6] **mystical** *adj.* inspiring a sense of mystery, awe, and fascination
[7] **inborn** *adj.* existing from birth
[8] **feat** *n.* a noteworthy act or accomplishment

out. He compared two calculating prodigies and two cashiers from a department store
in Paris. The cashiers had an average of fourteen years' experience in the store but had
shown no early gift for math. Binet gave the prodigies and the cashiers identical problems
and compared the time taken to solve them. What happened? The best cashier was faster
than either prodigy. Practice, on its own, was sufficient to bring "perfectly normal" people
up to and beyond the remarkable speed of prodigies.

None of this is to **deny** the idea of heredity or the principles of Darwinism. The evidence
shows that some kids start out better than others. But the key point is that the importance
of these initial differences disappears as the number of hours devoted to practice
increases. Over time, and with the right kind of practice, people can change so much.

None of this would matter terribly much if the question of talent was only theoretical.
But it is so much more than that. Consider someone who believes excellence is all about
talent (labeled the "fixed mindset"). Why would she bother to work hard? If she has the
right genes, won't she just cruise to the top? And if she lacks talent, well, why bother
at all? If, on the other hand, she really believes that effort trumps[9] talent (labeled the
"growth mindset"), she will not see failure as an indictment[10], but as an opportunity to
adapt and grow. And, if she is right, she will eventually succeed.

What a young person decides about the nature of talent, then, could scarcely be more
important. Think how often you hear people (particularly youngsters) say: "I lack the
brain for numbers," or "I don't have the coordination for sports." These beliefs are direct
manifestations[11] of the fixed mindset, and they destroy motivation. Those with a growth
mindset, on the other hand, do not regard their abilities as set in genetic stone. These are
the people who approach tasks with enthusiasm.

So, how can people **orient** themselves and their children to the growth mindset? How
can the power of motivation be unlocked? A few years ago, Carol Dweck, a leading
psychologist, took 400 students and gave them a simple puzzle. Afterward, each of the
students was given six words of praise. Half were praised for intelligence; the other half
were praised for effort. The results were remarkable. After the first test, the students were
given a choice of whether to take a hard or an easy test. A full two-thirds praised for
intelligence chose the easy task: they did not want to risk losing their "smart" label. But
ninety percent of the effort-praised group chose the tough test: they wanted to prove
just how hardworking they were. Then, the experiment gave the students a chance to
take a test of equal difficulty to the first test. The group praised for intelligence showed a
twenty percent decline in performance compared with the first test, even though it was
no harder. But the effort-praised group increased their score by thirty percent: failure had
actually spurred them on[12]. "These were some of the clearest findings I've seen," Dweck
said. "Praising children's intelligence harms motivation, and it harms performance."

Intelligence-based praise orients the receiver toward the fixed mindset; it suggests to
them that intelligence is of primary importance rather than the effort through which
intelligence can be transformed. This reveals a radical new approach to the way we
engage with children and each other: that we should praise effort, not talent; that we
should teach kids to see challenges as learning opportunities rather than as threats;
that we should emphasise how abilities can be transformed. When parents and teachers
adopt this approach—and stick to it—the results are remarkable.

---

[9] **trump** *v.* to beat (someone or something) by
doing something better
[10] **indictment** *n.* a sign that something is bad

[11] **manifestation** *n.* a sign that clearly shows
something; one form or instance of something
[12] **spur (someone) on** *idiom* to cause to work
harder or move faster

Q What is the relationship
between practice and early
differences in ability between
individuals? Underline the
information.

C Underline the definitions of
"fixed mindset" and "growth
mindset" in this paragraph.

C What is the author's main
purpose in this passage?
(1) To inform
(2) To entertain
(3) To convince

FOCUS ON CONTENT

Choose the best answer.

1 What is the main point of the passage?

    a. Children who think talent is developed through practice perform better and are more motivated.

    b. The idea that talent is hereditary can have negative effects.

    c. The abilities of prodigies come from practice, not inborn.

    d. Several studies show that practice cannot fully account for exceptional talent.

2 What kind of support does the author mainly give for his opinion?

    a. Research studies   b. Interviews with experts

    c. Explanations and definitions   d. Personal experience

3 Why does the author mention Rudiger Gamm?

    a. To give an example of a prodigy whose abilities regular people can never hope to match

    b. To demonstrate how the importance of hard work is often overlooked

    c. To prove that math prodigies need less practice than most people do

    d. To illustrate the importance of inborn ability

4 Why does the author think the question of talent is not merely theoretical?

    a. Because it is an issue that is still not easily settled

    b. Because it influences the thinking of teachers and coaches

    c. Because it is the topic of ongoing research

    d. Because it has a direct effect on students' attitudes and performance

5 Which of the following statements would the author most likely agree with?

    a. Teachers have to promote a fixed mindset among their students.

    b. Teachers with a growth mindset have a negative effect on students' performance.

    c. Teachers ought to praise students' hard work rather than their abilities.

    d. Teachers should choose which mindset they want to orient students to.

IDEAS IN ACTION

Talk about the questions with a partner.

1   What are some talents that you have which you'd like to develop more? How could you develop them?

2   Based on the examples of talented people you know, what do you think of the author's opinion? Do you agree or disagree with him? Why?

CRITICAL THINKING

Evaluation

Identifying Causation and Correlation

It is wrong to assume that just because two things occur at the same time, or one right after the other, that there must be a link between them. Readers must be cautious about these kinds of claims. When two trends occur together, it is called a **correlation**. Sometimes, there is a cause-and-effect relationship between the trends; sometimes, there is not. For example:

> As chess players spend more time analyzing their game, they win more matches.

Here, there's a clear cause-and-effect relationship. In some cases, though, there is no causal link between two things. For example:

> Many chess grandmasters are also skilled at mathematics.

Does that mean that one causes the other? Clearly not. It's much more likely that a third element causes both (perhaps skill in analyzing and predicting patterns).

Here are some questions to ask to help you work out the relationship between trends:

- Are the patterns or trends coincidental (i.e., correlation)? Or are they directly linked?
- Are they directly linked by cause and effect (i.e., causation)?
- Are they linked by a third cause?

Read the excerpts from Reading 2. Complete each sentence and evaluate the relationship between the trends with a partner.

1   None of this is to deny the idea of heredity or the principles of Darwinism. The evidence shows that some kids start out better than others. But the key point is that the importance of these initial differences disappears as the number of hours devoted to practice increases. Over time, and with the right kind of practice, people can change so much.

As the number of hours that kids practice increases, _____.

a. The trends are . . .   ☐ coincidental   ☐ directly linked

b. Are they linked by cause and effect?   ☐ Yes   ☐ No

c. Is there a third cause? If so, what is it?   _____

2 A few years ago, Carol Dweck, a leading psychologist, took 400 students and gave them a simple puzzle. Afterward, each of the students was given six words of praise. Half were praised for intelligence; the other half were praised for effort. The results were remarkable. After the first test, the students were given a choice of whether to take a hard or an easy test. A full two-thirds praised for intelligence chose the easy task: they did not want to risk losing their "smart" label. But ninety percent of the effort-praised group chose the tough test: they wanted to prove just how hardworking they were. Then, the experiment gave the students a chance to take a test of equal difficulty to the first test. The group praised for intelligence showed a twenty percent decline in performance compared with the first test, even though it was no harder. But the effort-praised group increased their score by thirty percent: failure had actually spurred them on.

When students are praised for effort, _____.

a. The trends are . . .   ☐ coincidental   ☐ directly linked

b. Are they linked by cause and effect?   ☐ Yes   ☐ No

c. Is there a third cause? If so, what is it?   _____

VOCABULARY REVIEW

1 **Match each word to its definition.**

1 compute (v.)   •   • **a** the relationship in size between one thing or part and another

2 deny (v.)   •   • **b** to continue to exist

3 imply (v.)   •   • **c** to find a value, usually by using mathematics

4 infer (v.)   •   • **d** to say something didn't happen or isn't true

5 initial (adj.)   •   • **e** to point in a certain direction; to align in relation to something

6 orient (v.)   •   • **f** to mean something without saying it directly

7 persist (v.)   •   • **g** to conclude that something is true based on indirect information

8 proportion (n.) •   • **h** during a period or stage near the beginning

2 **Fill in the blanks with the correct words from above.**

1 We made a(n) _____ guess based on earlier research, and our study later confirmed it.

2 The correct _____ is two parts lithium disulfide to three parts hydrogen peroxide.

3 She doesn't _____ that a mistake was made; however, she claims she was not the only one at fault.

4 Based on this data, researchers are able to _____ the average distance the whales travel annually to mate.

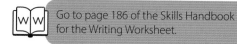
Go to page 186 of the Skills Handbook for the Writing Worksheet.

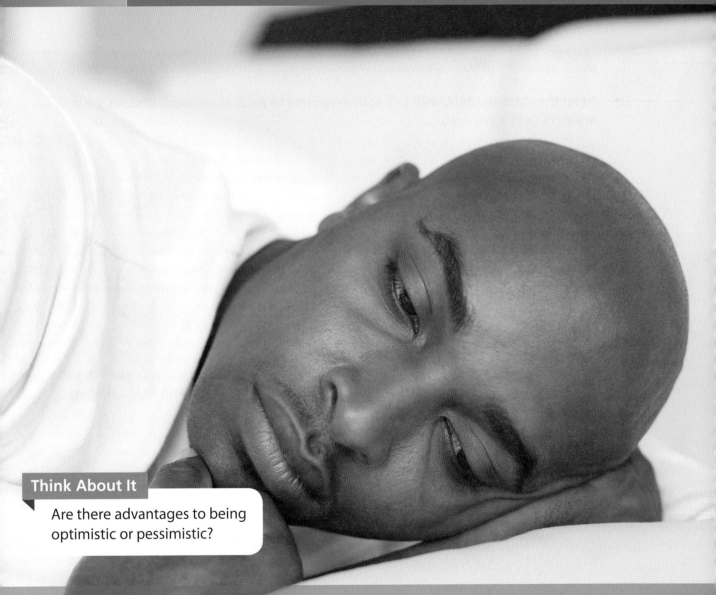

UNIT

8

Always Think Positive—or Not

How your outlook on life affects you

Think About It

Are there advantages to being optimistic or pessimistic?

There is no sadder sight than a young pessimist,
except an old optimist.

Mark Twain

Reading 1 / How Being an Optimist or a Pessimist Affects Your Health
Reading Skill: Determining Importance

Reading 2 / Hooray for Pessimism
Critical Thinking Skill: Recognizing Common Fallacies: Arguments from Ignorance

Unit Project | **Make Your Point**
Express your opinion about being an optimist or a pessimist

Before You Read

1 **Read the statements. Check (✔) your response to each statement. Discuss your answers with a partner.**

	Strongly disagree	Disagree somewhat	Agree somewhat	Strongly agree
1. I always focus on the positive side of things.				
2. In uncertain times, I usually expect the best.				
3. I'm excited about my future.				
4. Things usually work out the way I want them to.				

2 **Work out your score by adding up the values for your answers. The higher the score, the more optimistic you are (4 = least optimistic; 16 = most optimistic). Discuss these questions with a partner.**

- What is your score? Do you think it accurately reflect your character? Explain.
- Would you want to change your result if you could? Why or why not?

Reading 1

VOCABULARY PREVIEW

Read the sentence. Circle the choice that is closest to the meaning of the AWL word in bold.

1 Having a positive attitude can **dramatically** affect one's well-being.
   a. greatly   b. suddenly   c. easily

2 Optimists live with the **assumption** that everything will work out.
   a. hope   b. goal   c. belief

3 Those who score high on **assessments** of optimism have better moods.
   a. exercises   b. definitions   c. tests

4 The belief that pessimists are in worse health isn't entirely **unfounded**.
   a. unknown   b. unjustified   c. unbelievable

5 When pessimists become ill, their **recovery** tends to take longer.
   a. getting better   b. seeking help   c. showing symptoms

6 Negative people had a lower risk of death over a **projected** ten-year period.
   a. past   b. forecast   c. typical

7 Optimists may be **insufficiently** worried about the future.
   a. not often   b. not very   c. not enough

8 Optimism can lead people to **rationalize** risky behavior such as smoking.
   a. think about   b. find reasons for   c. be afraid of

READING PREVIEW

This passage is an online magazine article about how a positive or negative view of life impacts well-being.

> How might being an optimist affect your health positively? Negatively? What about being a pessimist? Discuss your ideas with a partner.

positive mental attitude

Read the online magazine article.

Track 15

How Being an Optimist or a Pessimist Affects Your Health

by Hope Gillette
© 2013, Voxxi.com. Used by permission.

We all know the eternal[1] optimist and the perpetual[2] pessimist, and chances are you've had your share of frustration with one or both personalities. But aside from how optimist or pessimist personalities affect other people, how do they affect those who actually embody[3] those traits? Are there health benefits—or disadvantages—to being perpetually positive or negative? 5

The Optimist Personality

It turns out that a positive outlook[4] can **dramatically** affect one's health. "Optimism may help you live longer and better in numerous ways. Research has shown that habitual optimists are less likely to develop depression and die from heart disease than pessimists, for example," says Linda Wasmer Andrews, a health writer with a master's degree in 10 psychology.

"That's partly because optimists are better at coping with setbacks and hardships," she adds. "When faced with a tough situation, optimists tend to respond with active problem-solving, positive thinking, and a sense of humor. Pessimists, on the other hand, tend to respond with hopelessness, denial, and avoidance. In the long run, this 15 difference in coping style may mean that optimists experience less stress than pessimists do." Positive thinking is crucial to stress management, and going through life with the **assumption** that things will work out has numerous long-term health benefits. These include: lower rates of depression, improved coping skills, and reduced risk of death from cardiovascular[5] disease. 20

"There are many health benefits to being optimistic," states psychologist Jaime Booth Cundy, who writes for *Psychology Today*. "There are a few studies that show that an optimistic outlook can help to prevent the common cold. More importantly, however, in my opinion, is the placebo[6] effect. The belief that you are going to get better is almost as powerful as many common cold remedies." 25

Thomas Plante, Ph.D., director of the Spirituality and Health Institute at Santa Clara University, agrees that being optimistic can be good for a person's health. Those who score high on **assessments** of optimism "tend to cope better with stress, have more social support (i.e., caring friends and family), be in better moods, and have more active and health-promoting coping styles," he explains. "Research also tells us that they tend to recover more quickly from some illnesses, have less pain post-surgery in general, show lower blood pressure, and so forth." 30

Optimists benefit from a stronger social support system.

Q Underline how optimists and pessimists cope with problems.

C What could be an objection to the argument that optimism leads to good health?

(1) It could be that it is good health that causes a person to be optimistic.

(2) It is possible that the health effects are not real but only imagined.

---

[1] **eternal** *adj.* having no end; lasting forever
[2] **perpetual** *adj.* constant; eternal
[3] **embody** *v.* to represent in human form; to have

[4] **outlook** *n.* a person's general attitude to life
[5] **cardiovascular** *adj.* related to the heart and blood vessels
[6] **placebo** *n.* a pill that has no physical effect but which the patient believes is a medicine

The Pessimist Personality

As pessimism is associated with negativity, it is natural to assume that pessimistic people are more prone[7] to poor health outcomes. As the research discussed above suggests, this conclusion is not entirely **unfounded**. But it is not true in all cases.

"Optimists tend to take better care of their own health," says Andrews. "They genuinely believe that what they eat, how much they exercise, and how well they work with their doctor can make a positive difference. In contrast, pessimists . . . believe there's nothing they can do to change fate. So why bother improving their diet, going to the gym, or sticking with a disease management plan?"

Experts agree that too much pessimism can lead to hypochondria—the tendency to believe that a disease is present when it really is not. However, being a pessimist may provide an advantage when it comes to health prevention. "A pessimist is more likely to seek the advice of a professional. While in extreme cases this could lead to hypochondria, it could also lead to a potentially life-saving diagnosis[8]," Cundy points out. "Pessimism affects the body the same way the placebo effect would. It is just goes the other way. If a placebo can make someone believe that they are getting better and they do, then the thought that you are sick can actually make you sicker."

Q Underline the information that shows the contrast between the placebo effect and the effect that negative thoughts have on the body.

Plante notes that pessimism is still linked to a number of negative health effects, including poorer mood, less social support, prolonged[9] **recovery** from stress and illness, and less satisfaction with life. However, in the long run, pessimists may in some cases live longer than their optimistic counterparts.

C Is the argument in this paragraph inductive or deductive?

A 2013 study published by the American Psychological Association suggests that pessimistic people had a lower risk of death over a **projected** ten-year period compared to people who were more positive. "Pessimism about the future may encourage people to live more carefully, taking health and safety precautions," says lead author Frieder Lang, a professor at the University of Erlangen-Nuremberg in Germany.

Andrews notes that there are certainly health disadvantages to being **insufficiently** worried about the future. It can cause someone to **rationalize** risky behavior, for instance. "Let's say you're a smoker," she explains. "It's unrealistically optimistic to think that lung cancer, heart disease, and COPD[10] could never happen to you. And that belief may lead you to keep smoking."

Middle Ground

Both optimism and pessimism can impact health, but it seems both personalities could use a little bit of one another to really keep an individual at peak health. The optimist needs the caution of the pessimist, and the pessimist needs the drive of the optimist. "My father has always considered himself a 'guarded optimist'," says Cundy. "He explains it this way: An optimist approaches a stop sign at a one way and only looks right. . . A guarded optimist will approach the stop sign and look both ways not really expecting to see anyone—but, hey, how hard is it to look both ways?"

What's more, all three experts agree that a pessimist who actively works toward being optimistic can enjoy the health benefits linked to having an upbeat personality. "There are exceptions to every rule," states Andrews. "But for most people most of the time, it seems to be healthiest to put on neither rose-colored glasses[11] nor mud-colored ones, but rather glasses with good, clear lenses."

C The last sentence of the passage is a generalization. Circle the qualifying language.

---

7 **prone** *adj.* likely; susceptible
8 **diagnosis** *n.* the identification of a disease
9 **prolonged** *adj.* lasting a long time

10 **COPD** (chronic obstructive pulmonary disease) *n.* a disease of the lungs that causes breathing difficulty
11 **rose-colored glasses** *idiom* a naively optimistic view of things

103

MAPPING IDEAS

Organize the ideas from Reading 1. Review the passage and fill in the graphic organizer below.

> **How optimism and pessimism affect your health**

Effects of Optimism
- Better at coping with [1] _____
- More social support
- Recover [2] _____ from illness
- Lower risk of depression, fatal heart disease
- May rationalize unhealthy behavior

Effects of Pessimism
- Don't think they can [3] _____, so may not bother trying
- Reverse placebo effect
- More likely to seek [4] _____
- May live longer because they are more cautious

> The healthiest attitude may be described as "[5] _____ optimism."

> R W   Before you go on, boost your reading skills. Go to page 187 of the Skills Handbook.

FOCUS ON CONTENT

Comprehension

❶ **Circle the main idea of the passage below. For each of the other sentences, check the reason it is not the main idea.**

1 Being pessimistic is bad for one's health in every way.

☐ too general   ☐ too specific   ☐ not in passage   ☐ inaccurate

2 Pessimists have a higher risk of some health problems than optimists do.

☐ too general   ☐ too specific   ☐ not in passage   ☐ inaccurate

3 To help their patients, doctors should encourage them to be more optimistic.

☐ too general   ☐ too specific   ☐ not in passage   ☐ inaccurate

4 Both optimism and pessimism are associated with good and bad health effects.

☐ too general   ☐ too specific   ☐ not in passage   ☐ inaccurate

2 **Check the statements that are true according to the passage. Correct the false statements.**

1 ☐ Pessimists respond to problems by actively looking for solutions.

_____

2 ☐ Some research says optimists are less likely to catch the common cold.

_____

3 ☐ A 2013 study showed a higher risk of death for pessimists.

_____

4 ☐ Excessive optimism might prevent someone from quitting smoking.

_____

3 **Choose the best answer.**

1 Which of the following is NOT mentioned in paragraph 5 as a benefit of optimism?

    a. Better at managing stress
    b. Easier recovery from surgery
    c. More physical activity
    d. A fuller social life

2 What can be inferred about Cundy from the second-to-last paragraph?

    a. She thinks her father has the correct attitude.
    b. She is more pessimistic than her father.
    c. Her father convinced her to study psychology.
    d. Her father has had a lot of health problems.

THINK AND DISCUSS

 Application

1 **Read the excerpt from the reading passage.**

How Being an Optimist or a Pessimist Affects Your Health

We all know the eternal optimist and the perpetual pessimist, and chances are you've had your share of frustration with one or both personalities.

Discuss the following questions with a partner.

- Think of someone you know who is either extremely optimistic or extremely pessimistic. Explain how he or she demonstrates this attitude.
- In what way(s) can optimists be frustrating for other people? What about pessimists?

② **Read the descriptions of the two people below. Which of them has an attitude that is more likely to promote good health and a long life? Write a brief explanation of your choice.**

Jun
- Has very little stress
- Expects only good things to happen to him
- Smokes but believes it will be easy to quit

_____

_____

_____

_____

Sophie
- Dislikes exercise but does it anyway
- Complains to her friends when stressed
- Worries about cancer because it runs in her family

_____

_____

_____

_____

VOCABULARY REVIEW

Fill in the blanks with the correct words from the box. Change the form of the word if necessary.

assumption	recovery	insufficiently	projected
unfounded	assessment	dramatically	rationalize

1 Many experts do not consider IQ tests to be valid _____ of intelligence.

2 You won't get the job if you seem _____ interested in it.

3 The senator assured the public that the accusations against her were _____.

4 Many arguments are based on one or more unstated _____.

5 The economy's _____ from the financial crisis has been slow.

6 This report includes data on our past, current, and _____ expenses.

7 I tried to _____ her bad temper by telling myself she was just stressed out.

8 This area has changed _____, from mostly rural to mostly urban.

Reading 2

VOCABULARY PREVIEW

Match each AWL word with its meaning from the box.

> a. relating to the use of machines
> b. fake but made to seem real
> c. the chances of something happening; probability
> d. reasonable
> e. the state of being the most influential or powerful
> f. a future chance; an opportunity for the future
> g. a reason for doing something
> h. to move forward; to continue

_____ **1** I am not usually hopeful about my **prospects** of a bright future.

_____ **2** Against the **odds**, sometimes good things do happen.

_____ **3** Stress about the future can be a **motivation** to act.

_____ **4** You might expect **technical** problems with your computer.

_____ **5** People who think everything will **proceed** smoothly might not prepare for problems.

_____ **6** One experiment involved students playing **simulated** card games.

_____ **7** Lowering your bets after losing is a **logical** thing to do.

_____ **8** The **dominance** of optimism in our culture may come to an end soon.

READING PREVIEW

This passage is an essay about the possible advantages of being a pessimist.

In what kinds of situations can expecting the worst be helpful? Think of at least one example and discuss it with a partner.

Read the essay.

Hooray for Pessimism

by Regina Lalonde

"Think positive!" "Look on the bright side!" "Smile! Everything will work out in the end!" These words of advice—commands, really—come my way on a regular basis, from family, friends, co-workers, and even total strangers. You see, I'm a pessimist. I wouldn't describe myself as unhappy; however, at any given moment, I'm more likely to be frowning in thought about what might go wrong next than I am to be smiling at the **prospect** of a 5 bright future. This puts me in the minority in a culture that practically worships positive thinking. Hence, the constant orders from those around me to be more optimistic. Since pessimism is in my nature, I couldn't obey them if I wanted to. But I don't want to. Despite the social and health benefits of optimism, which are no doubt real to some degree, I've learned that pessimism is greatly underrated[1]. A healthy amount of such negativity can 10 actually benefit a person emotionally, professionally, and financially.

Pessimism takes many forms, but the relevant ones here are dispositional and defensive pessimism. (Think "disposition" as in "personality.") In psychology, dispositional pessimism is the personality trait of having generally low expectations. In other words, a dispositional pessimist may not know what's going to happen, but he or she is pretty sure it won't be 15 anything great.

Although this sounds like a dreary[2] way to go through life, dispositional pessimism might lead to stronger, longer-lasting relationships. Several recent studies have found that negativity has a positive effect on couples because it prepares them for the worst. One study followed eighty-two married couples and found that when they encountered difficulties it was the optimists that suffered most because their disappointment was "extreme and often irrational." By

Couples with lower expectations seem to deal with conflict better.

trying to be relentlessly[3] positive, they actually harmed their relationships. In contrast, 25 the dispositional pessimists accepted some trouble as normal, and thus were able to deal with it. According to the lead researcher, these couples ended up with more successful and satisfying marriages as a result.

A bit of dispositional pessimism comes in handy at work as well. Dr. Aaron Sackett, Ph.D., is a psychologist at the University of St. Thomas in St. Paul and a critic of what he calls 30 the "cult[4]" of optimism. As he explained to *Psychology Today*, if an optimist is denied an expected promotion, he or she will feel both shocked and crushed. A pessimist in the same situation never had his or her hopes up[5] to begin with, and therefore will not be nearly so deeply affected. Pessimists, then, have built-in ego protection. Since disappointment is

Q Why does the author describe herself as "in the minority"?

C Circle the term that is defined in this paragraph. Underline the definition.

Q The author uses a hypothetical situation to illustrate the point of this paragraph. Underline it.

---

[1] **underrated** *adj.* not valued enough

[2] **dreary** *adj.* depressing

[3] **relentlessly** *adv.* without stopping or giving up

[4] **cult** *n.* a false and often dangerous religion

[5] **get / have one's hopes up** *idiom* to become hopeful

inevitable in any career, the pessimist's way does appear wiser. As a bonus, pessimists are especially delighted when, against all **odds**, good things do happen. "Optimists never get the joy of a pleasant surprise," Sackett points out.

Defensive pessimism benefits people in more concrete[6] ways. It is useful to view it as dispositional pessimism applied to specific situations: It is the tendency to be anxious about what could go wrong and to use that anxiety as **motivation** to act.

The advantages of this in the workplace are pretty obvious. Say you are a pessimist in charge of organizing an important presentation. You'll expect **technical** problems, so you'll set up and test the computer equipment in advance. You'll fear that additional people might show up, so you'll have extra copies of the handouts ready. And you'll worry that the meeting will run longer than expected, so you'll arrange for snacks to be delivered. Through the power of negative thinking, you will be much better prepared than the optimist who assumes everything will **proceed** smoothly. Now, granted, research suggests that optimists are more likely to be hired and are quicker to be promoted. To me,

this merely confirms what I already knew—that people usually prefer being around optimists because of their sunny personalities. Significantly, what this research does not prove is that a positive outlook actually makes someone a better or more efficient worker. The opposite seems more likely to be true.

Optimistic gamblers are sure they'll win—even when they're losing.

Defensive pessimism seems to lead to more prudent[7] money management, too. One interesting experiment involved observing college students as they gambled at **simulated** card games and slot machines. Those who had scored high on a test of optimism were more likely to believe they would win—and they believed this even more strongly after they had lost money— leading to further losses. Only the pessimistic students reduced their bets after losing, which is surely the **logical** thing to do. A similar principle could be observed on a global scale following the 2008 world financial crisis, which made defensive pessimists out of millions of people. Since then, people in many affected countries have felt increased anxiety about their financial futures and have adjusted their behavior accordingly, saving more for retirement and avoiding disastrous credit card debt.

Considering how pessimism can prevent disappointment, shield[8] one's ego, and protect against job-related or financial misfortunes, one would think it would be more widely accepted. Dr. Julie Norem, Ph.D., who specializes in this area told the *Huffington Post*: "There's an awful lot of pressure for people to present themselves as optimistic, and it probably causes more pain than the pessimism itself." Norem adds that the **dominance** of optimism may be coming to an end, and soon there may be a "broad cultural shift" toward more negativity. Maybe, but I'm not getting my hopes up.

C The author raises a possible objection to the argument in this paragraph. Underline it.

C Is the argument in this paragraph inductive or deductive?

---

[6] **concrete** *adj.* involving specific people, situations, etc., and not ideas or qualities

[7] **prudent** *adj.* careful and sensible

[8] **shield** *v.* to protect

FOCUS ON CONTENT

① **Choose the best answer.**

Comprehension

1 What is the main idea of paragraph 3?
    a. Married couples usually become more pessimistic over time.
    b. Pessimism helps relationships by keeping expectations realistic.
    c. Pessimists are more cautious about whom they marry.
    d. Most newly married couples are optimistic about the future.

2 According to paragraph 4, pessimists are _____.
    a. less likely to have big egos
    b. less likely to ask for promotions
    c. more likely to be promoted
    d. more happily surprised when things go well

3 What can be inferred about defensive pessimism?
    a. It is useful in stressful situations.
    b. It is generally only displayed at work.
    c. It may be a disadvantage in one's social life.
    d. It is less common than dispositional pessimism.

4 According to paragraph 6, studies show that optimists _____.
    a. stay at the same job longer
    b. are preferred by employers
    c. take more risks in their careers
    d. have poorer job performance on average

5 According to paragraph 7, what has the 2008 financial crisis demonstrated?
    a. The impossibility of predicting economic trends
    b. The difficulty of changing one's money habits
    c. The benefits of defensive pessimism
    d. The carelessness of most optimists

② **Complete the sentences with information from the passage.**

1 Optimistic couples who had problems felt _____.

2 Dispositional pessimism can protect one's _____ by being less affected by disappointments.

3 Defensive pessimism means that if something goes wrong, the pessimist _____.

4 Optimistic gamblers were found to be even more confident after _____.

IDEAS IN ACTION

Talk about the questions with a partner.

1 In what ways do you think being a pessimist can be harmful to a career?

2 Think of the last time you had to do something stressful. Did you practice "defensive pessimism"?
Explain.

CRITICAL THINKING

Recognizing Common Fallacies: Arguments from Ignorance

An **argument from ignorance**, also known as an **appeal to ignorance**, is a common type of invalid argument. Put simply, it is the argument that something must be true because there is no evidence that it is not true. It results from confusing a lack of evidence with impossibility. One way to remember this fallacy is: absence of evidence does not equal evidence of absence.

Arguments from ignorance usually take either of these logical forms:

> A *is true because it has not been proven false.*
> A *is false because it has not been proven true.*

For example:

> No one has produced evidence that there is life on other planets. Therefore, aliens do not exist.
> What I saw in the sky was an alien spaceship. No one has been able to prove that it wasn't.

A variation of this fallacy is an **argument from personal conviction**. In this case, the writer's personal belief (or inability to believe something) is presented as proof:

> The idea of aliens is just ridiculous. I don't see how they could possibly exist.

---

1 **Read the excerpt from Reading 2. Underline the argument from ignorance.**

> The advantages of this in the workplace are pretty obvious. Say you are a pessimist in charge of organizing an important presentation. You'll expect technical problems, so you'll set up and test the computer equipment in advance. You'll fear that additional people might show up, so you'll have extra copies of the handouts ready. And you'll worry that the meeting will run longer than expected, so you'll arrange for snacks to be delivered. Through the power of negative thinking, you will be much better prepared than the optimist who assumes everything will proceed smoothly. Now, granted, research suggests that optimists are more likely to be hired and are quicker to be promoted. To me, this merely confirms what I already knew—that people usually prefer being around optimists because of their sunny personalities. Significantly, what this research does not prove is that a positive outlook actually makes someone a better or more efficient worker. The opposite seems more likely to be true.

② **Read the following arguments and label them as arguments from ignorance (I), arguments from personal conviction (C), or supported arguments (S).**

1 I believe a link exists between outlook and athletic performance as well. Obviously, athletes with optimistic outlooks will outperform athletes with pessimistic outlooks. Arguing the opposite just does not make sense. _____

2 Although one's outlook can affect performance at work, the same is not true for performance at school. While studies show that optimistic employees tend to advance more frequently than pessimistic employees, no studies exist to show that optimistic students score higher on exams. Thus, there is no link between outlook and academic performance. _____

3 A positive correlation exists between pessimism and healthy diet choices. A survey conducted by Oxford University researchers found that pessimists tend to worry more about the effects of dietary choices. Therefore, they purchase fruits, vegetables, and other healthy items at a rate nearly double that of optimistic shoppers. _____

VOCABULARY REVIEW

Fill in the blanks with the correct words from the box. Change the form of the words if necessary.

technical	dominance	motivation	logical
prospect	simulated	proceed	odds

1 You can take a five-minute break now, after which the exam will _____.

2 It's possible to get an upgrade to first class if you ask for one, but the _____ are against it.

3 Because of his _____ knowledge, Ted is the one we go to with our computer problems.

4 The chimpanzees live in a(n) _____ jungle environment at the zoo.

5 Why do you think soccer has achieved _____ among all the world's sports?

6 People don't always make _____ decisions when they are very tired or upset.

7 When training your dog, use its favorite treats as _____.

8 The _____ of a long, cold winter is not appealing to me.

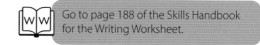
Go to page 188 of the Skills Handbook for the Writing Worksheet.

Coming Home Again

Why more young adults are moving back in with their parents

Think About It

Is it a good idea for people in their twenties and thirties to live with their parents?

There's a difference between immaturity and not being ready, and there's a certain maturity in admitting that you're not ready.

Aprille Legacy

Reading 1 / Generation Boomerang: Children Who Go Back to Mom and Dad
Reading Skill: Monitoring and Clarifying Understanding

Reading 2 / Boomerang Kids and Living Independently
Critical Thinking Skill: Classifying Claims

Unit Project | **Make Your Point**
Express your opinion about adults living with their parents

Before You Read

❶ Answer the questions. Discuss your answers with a partner.

1 When do you think young adults should start living on their own?
    a. As soon as legally possible   b. By about 25   c. When they get married   d. Other

2 Do today's young people take longer to grow up than previous generations did?
    a. Yes   b. No   c. In some ways

3 In your culture, is it considered embarrassing for people to live with their parents in their twenties or thirties?
    a. Yes   b. No   c. Depends

❷ The charts below show information about American adults between 18 and 31 years of age. Discuss the questions with a partner.

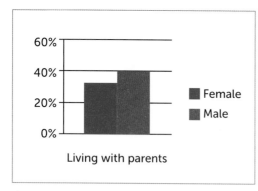

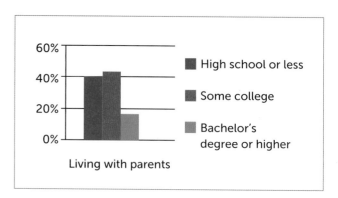

Source: pewsocialtrends.org, 2012

- Are any of the statistics surprising to you? Why or why not?
- Do you think these charts would look very different if they were about your country?

Reading 1

VOCABULARY PREVIEW

Read the sentence. Circle the choice that is closest to the meaning of the AWL word in bold.

1 Today's students will finish college with **unprecedented** levels of debt.
   a. hard to imagine
   b. never seen before
   c. impossible to pay

2 Lending **institutions** are more cautious about offering mortgages.
   a. organizations
   b. financial regulations
   c. experts

3 It's comforting for young people to move in with their **devoted** parents.
   a. familiar
   b. happy
   c. loving

4 Living with parents might prevent a person from reaching true **maturity**.
   a. adulthood
   b. satisfaction
   c. success

5 People cannot be **reliant** on their moms and dads forever.
   a. critical
   b. similar
   c. dependent

6 Parents provide their children with **stability**.
   a. the state of being wealthy
   b. the state of being unchanging
   c. the state of being confident

7 Boomerang kids might feel bad about **imposing** on their parents.
   a. asking for money
   b. arguing with
   c. causing inconvenience

8 The rent that boomerang kids pay their parents may not be enough to cover food and **utilities**.
   a. electricity, water, etc.
   b. TV, newspapers, etc.
   c. food, clothes, etc.

 Before you go on, boost your reading skills. Go to page 190 of the Skills Handbook.

READING PREVIEW

This passage is an online magazine article about young adults in the UK who are moving back in with their parents.

What problems do you think could occur when adults live with their parents? Think of at least two and discuss them with a partner.

Generation Boomerang: Children Who Go Back to Mom and Dad

by Sally Koslow and Hannah Booth
© 2012, Guardian News & Media Ltd. Used by permission.

When my husband and I learned that, at 25, one son would be returning to live with us again, we initially expected his stay to last perhaps two months. Then he lost his job. Months passed, and we found ourselves unable to stay silent. "Have you updated your résumé? While you're at it, could you please do your laundry, clean up, and walk the dog?" Eventually, with a shove[1], our son reluctantly accepted a job and moved out. 5

A decade later, the number of "adultescents" living in their parents' homes has increased apace[2], victims of a slow economy. According to the Office for National Statistics, nearly three million British adults aged 20 to 34 lived with their parents in 2011, up twenty percent since 1997. More than one million under-25s are now unemployed; and with the introduction of higher tuition fees, future students should expect to finish their degree 10 with **unprecedented** debts of up to £60,000. Lending **institutions** are shying away from offering mortgages[3], and house prices have risen beyond the realms[4] of possibility for many young people.

Q Underline all the reasons given in the paragraph why young British people are struggling financially.

These experiences may result in a severe hit to self-esteem; returning home to **devoted** parents can sometimes 15 soothe[5] that wound. Many young adults, however, exist in a cloud of overconfidence, with an illusion of endless time. "This is a more entitled generation than their parents' and grandparents,'" says William J. Doherty, professor of family social science. "We're seeing young adults tethered[6] to 20 family in the sense that they live at home, but with no major responsibility to work as contributing members."

Boomerang kids might view living at home as a long vacation.

Q What adjective is used to describe the young generation in this paragraph? Circle it.

Today's parents tend to treat young adults like pampered[7] teens, reinvesting in dormant[8] parenting roles, especially if their kids are struggling. "The underlying message is 'We don't think you can do it on your own,'" says Marie Hartwell-Walker, psychologist and 25 mother of four adult children, two of whom came home to live with her and her husband. This treatment prevents their kids from truly reaching **maturity**.

C Underline an appeal to authority in the first half of the passage.

It's painful to recognize that adults cannot be **reliant** on their parents forever, and that many life lessons must be learned alone. This truth is compounded by baby boomers'[9] refusal to acknowledge getting older, which sends an additional message to young 30

---

[1] **shove** *n.* a push
[2] **apace** *adv.* quickly
[3] **mortgage** *n.* a loan to buy a home
[4] **realm** *n.* an area of activity, influence, etc.
[5] **soothe** *v.* to cause pain to go away; to relieve
[6] **tether** *v.* to tie

[7] **pampered** *adj.* treated with a lot of attention and care
[8] **dormant** *adj.* temporarily inactive
[9] **baby boomer** *n.* a member of the "baby boom" generation, the unusually large generation born after World War II

adults that there will always be time to get another degree, to break up with one more partner or employer, or to change direction. If parents aren't "old" (and with hair color and joint replacements, who doesn't want to pretend they're still 40?), then for adultescents, the years must be standing still. Parents of adult children need to step back so young
35 adults can step forward.

Gareth Johnson, 38, lives with his parents and his nephew in south London

Gareth says: "My mum and dad are extremely supportive. They've never brought up the subject of me leaving. I'm unemployed—I got a master's in forensic art[10] a few years ago, but haven't found work in that area yet, even though I've applied for more than 300 jobs.

40 "Everything changed when my sister died suddenly six years ago. I had been considering moving out and that put a hold on things; it changed my whole perspective on life. I used to work in TV production design, and it made me want to do something more worthwhile, which is why I did my postgraduate degree.

Q Why did Gareth decide to get another degree?

"Mum and Dad are raising my nephew, Seth, and I'm a sort of dad/uncle/brother to him.
45 They provide him with **stability**, as they do for me. I get unemployment benefits, so I don't pay any rent. We eat together most evenings, but cooking is a bit of a problem: my mum and dad don't eat the sort of stuff I like, so they tend to do the cooking. Dad does most of the cleaning, but I do my own laundry and clean up after dinner. I don't get any teasing from my friends, as they've all done the back-to-home thing before."

50 *Gareth's father, Carl, says*: "If we had the money to set him up on his own, we would. Some members of our family think we're a bit too supportive and drop hints that Gareth should try to find a job, but we do like having him around. Like any family member, he has good and bad points: he's always leaving the lights on, but he brews fabulous beer. He and Seth get along wonderfully: they play football in the hall, just like Gareth did as a kid with
55 his own uncles."

Q Who is Seth, and why do you think he lives with Gareth's parents?

Michelle Nicoll, 27, and her husband David, 30, live with her parents in Essex

Michelle says: "David and I had been renting for two years before we got engaged and realized we'd never be able to afford a wedding and a deposit for a house while wasting money on rent. We had no savings; and though we didn't want a big wedding, we wanted
60 all the family there, so our only option was to move back in with my parents.

"It was depressing—I felt as if we were **imposing**, and that we'd failed. The hardest part was adjusting to my parents' routines. When we lived together, we did chores when we felt like it, and now we feel we have to wash up right after dinner, or tidy up when they want us to. Between us, David and I pay £225 a month in rent, which probably doesn't
65 even cover food or **utilities**."

Michelle's mother, Jan, says: "We thought, if we don't help Michelle and David out, there's no chance of them getting anywhere. Michelle and I are very different, and we have clashed[11], particularly in the kitchen. They have two cats and it took our dog a while to get used to them, and we had to work out timings for the bathroom in the morning, as
70 we have only one. For their sake, mostly, I'm looking forward to when they move out and can get their lives in order."

---

[10] **forensic art** *n.* the skills practiced by artists in police work, such as drawing suspects' faces

[11] **clash** *v.* to argue; to fight

MAPPING IDEAS

Organize the ideas from Reading 1. Review the passage and fill in the graphic organizer below.

Generation boomerang

Recent UK trends

- Number of adults living at home up by

  1 _____ since 1997

- Higher tuition leading to

  2 _____

- High unemployment and home prices

- Parents pamper them, so kids not mature

Gareth

- Parents very supportive

- Has applied for hundreds of jobs

- Parents also raising

  3 _____

- Does some chores

- Some relatives think

  4 _____

Michelle

- Married and saving money to buy 5 _____

- Trouble adjusting to

  6 _____

- Clashes with mother

- Mom can't wait for them to move out

FOCUS ON CONTENT

❶ **Circle the main idea of the passage. For each of the other sentences, check the reason it is not the main idea.**

1 Gareth Johnson and Michelle Nicoll regret moving back in with their parents.

☐ too general ☐ too specific ☐ not in passage ☐ inaccurate

2 Economic trends mean that many young people can't afford to buy homes.

☐ too general ☐ too specific ☐ not in passage ☐ inaccurate

3 More young adults are moving in with their parents, which has pros and cons.

☐ too general ☐ too specific ☐ not in passage ☐ inaccurate

4 Young people who live with their parents longer end up being more successful.

☐ too general ☐ too specific ☐ not in passage ☐ inaccurate

2 **Check the statements that are true according to the passage. Correct the false statements.**

1 The author's 25-year-old son moved out after he got a job.

_____

2 Professor Doherty thinks today's boomerang kids lack a sense of responsibility.

_____

3 Gareth's friends make fun of him for living with his parents.

_____

4 Michelle felt welcome when she and her husband moved in with her parents.

_____

3 **Choose the best answer.**

1 What can be inferred about baby boomers from paragraph 5?
   a. They wish their children were more independent.
   b. They want to see themselves as young.
   c. They were unusually dependent on their parents when young.
   d. They are better educated than their children are.

2 Which is NOT true about Michelle Nicoll and her husband?
   a. Her parents will be glad when they move out.
   b. They hadn't saved up any money before getting married.
   c. They wanted a large, expensive wedding.
   d. They pay rent to her parents.

THINK AND DISCUSS

Application

1 **Read the excerpt from the reading passage.**

Generation Boomerang: Children Who Go Back to Mom and Dad

Many young adults, however, exist in a cloud of overconfidence, with an illusion of endless time. "This is a more entitled generation than their parents' and grandparents,'" says William J. Doherty, professor of family social science.

Discuss the following questions with a partner.

• Do you agree that today's young generation is overconfident and more entitled than previous ones?
• In what other ways do you think young people today differ from their parents?

② Imagine a 28-year-old friend is moving in with her parents for financial reasons, after living independently for years. She feels a little depressed about it. What advice would you give her? Write her a short email.

Dear Tanya,

_____

_____

_____

_____

_____

_____

VOCABULARY REVIEW

① Match each word to its definition.

1 stability (n.) •	• **a**	an established organization
2 devoted (adj.) •	• **b**	happening for the first time
3 maturity (n.) •	• **c**	to force something unwelcome on
4 utility (n.) •	• **d**	the state of being emotionally grown up
5 impose (v.) •	• **e**	caring
6 reliant (adj.) •	• **f**	a public service such as power, gas, and water
7 unprecedented (adj.) •	• **g**	permanence
8 institution (n.) •	• **h**	needing someone or something for support

② Fill in the blanks with the correct words from above. Change the form of the word if necessary.

1 I hate to _____, but would you mind picking up my mail while I'm away?

2 Most countries are _____ on imported oil to meet their energy needs.

3 The billionaire used his money to found a(n) _____ for educating poor children.

4 Taking responsibility for one's mistakes is a sign of _____.

Reading 2

VOCABULARY PREVIEW

Match each AWL word in bold with its meaning from the box.

> a. to occur or be present at the same time
> b. to limit or restrict
> c. a change from one state or condition to another
> d. to erase, remove, or destroy
> e. to bring back; to return something to its earlier condition
> f. help
> g. a home
> h. to give a new meaning to

_____ **1** It is hard for many young people to **eliminate** their student loan debts.

_____ **2** A larger percentage of adults are living in their parents' **residence**.

_____ **3** Slow wage growth is **constraining** the choices of the young generation.

_____ **4** An increase in the unemployment rate **accompanied** the financial crisis.

_____ **5** It can be expensive to make the **transition** to living on your own.

_____ **6** Living with parents can help young adults **restore** their financial health.

_____ **7** More parents are providing financial **assistance** to their grown children who are hard up.

_____ **8** The young generation is **redefining** adulthood by moving back home.

READING PREVIEW

This essay is about why "boomerang kids" are becoming more common in Canada.

Why do you think the number of boomerang kids is growing? Think of at least two reasons and discuss them with a partner.

Boomerang Kids and Living Independently

Track 18

by Kelly Shepherd / Language Cradle Consulting

Jenny Currie is a 28-year-old graduate with a degree in English Literature from the University of British Columbia in Vancouver, Canada. She enjoyed her studies and aspires[1] to a career as a writer and educator. However, the economic situation in Burnaby, where she lives, is quite dismal[2]. Even with a steady job, she has discovered that it's practically impossible to afford her rent and expenses on top of trying to **eliminate** her student loan 5 debt. Her parents have suggested that, to **restore** her financial well-being, she should move to Calgary, Alberta, with them so that she can pay off her debt faster. Jenny is not alone in her predicament[3]. Gone are the days when children would leave the parental home for good as soon as they reached adulthood. Her generation is **redefining** the process of becoming an adult. 10

Q What is Jenny's main problem? Underline it.

Jenny is part of a segment of Canadian society that has been labeled the Boomerang Generation—those adults who move back home after living independently. However, Canada is not the only country to experience this. According to an article written by Lisa Smith for *Investopedia*, the Italians call these grown children "*mammon*, or mama's boys; the Japanese call them *parasaito shinguru*, or parasite singles." In 2012, a Pew Research 15 analysis noted that "the share of Americans living in multi-generational family households is the highest it has been since the 1950s." A large-scale study in the same year showed that about thirty-five percent of people between the ages of 18 and 31 were living at their parents' **residence**.

Slow wage growth for young people is making it hard for them to support themselves.

The main reason these grown children decide to go back home 20 is financial. As in Jenny's case, most boomerang kids are well-educated and enthusiastic to live independently. However, the wages they receive are simply insufficient to support them. According to Employment and Social Development Canada, between 1981 and 2011, "the proportion of young adults aged 20 25 to 29 who resided in their parental home rose fifteen percentage points from twenty-seven percent to forty-two percent." In their study for Statistics Canada, researchers Rene Morisett, Garnett Picot, and Yuqian Lu found that, from 1981 to 2011, average wages increased by seventeen percent among men aged 45 to 54 but only one percent 30 among men aged 25 to 34. Hourly wages for women aged 45 to 54 grew by thirty-three

C What causal argument does the author make in this paragraph?

---

[1] **aspire** *v.* to want to have or achieve
[2] **dismal** *adj.* very poor or bad
[3] **predicament** *n.* a difficult situation

percent, more than twice the fourteen-percent rate observed for younger women. The Boomerang Generation is **constrained** financially, as wage growth has stalled[4] in the past few decades. This means they have less ability to live without parental **assistance**.

35 Also, the ever-increasing expenses required to make the **transition** to an independent life add to the problem. Jenny is employed as a technical editor with an annual salary of $42,000 before taxes (which take up approximately a quarter of her income). Her rent is $1,200 a month for a one-bedroom apartment. She pays around $200 for extras like Internet and cable. Groceries cost her $300 a month on average, and she has a $500
40 student loan payment every month. Her high living expenses mean that she has very little left over. Moving back in with her parents would be a smart strategy to pay off her debt more quickly. Fortunately for Jenny, she has a job that travels with her wherever she goes, so she doesn't need to be in the office to work. This means she'll still be employed when she moves back in with her parents. However, more and more young people are
45 finding it difficult to gain any employment due to a worldwide economic slowdown.

Q Underline Jenny's four main expenses.

The job market has not fully recovered from the 2008 financial crisis.

The 2008 financial crisis in the US spread to all parts of the world, including Canada. An increase in the unemployment rate **accompanied** the crisis, and this caused consumer spending to decline. It also caused financial market
50 instability, and employers began downsizing[5]. According to Statistics Canada, in 2007, the unemployment rate was at a 33-year low of six percent. In 2009, it rose to 8.6 percent. It has dropped a little in recent years; but as the newer generations hit the job market, unemployment will very likely increase again in years to come. Couple that with
55 high student loans to pay off, and Jenny's move back home appears to be not only a wise financial move but a necessary one.

C What argument does the author make in this paragraph? Underline the conclusion.

The depletion[6] of employment possibilities, the heavy burden of student loan payments, and a high cost of living have created a difficult situation for people who are eager to achieve autonomy[7]. Does this mean that grown children may never leave the comfort
60 of their parental homes? Most boomerang adults have already made a reasonable effort to leave the family nest and regain independence. They probably see moving back with their parents as a last resort[9]. After paying off debts and establishing their careers, most adult children will want to strike out on their own again. Hopefully, the next decade will see more economic growth and employment stability to allow them to do so.

C This paragraph contains several generalizations. Underline at least one. Circle the qualifying language.

4   **stall** *v.* to stop
5   **downsize** *v.* to reduce the size of a company's staff
6   **depletion** *n.* decrease in quantity
7   **autonomy** *n.* independence; freedom
8   **resort** *n.* a resource used in desperate situations

FOCUS ON CONTENT

❶   Choose the best answer.

1 Which is NOT true about Jenny Currie, according to paragraph 1?
   a. She has a university degree.
   b. She is currently unemployed.
   c. She borrowed money for her education.
   d. She has been advised by her parents to move in with them.

2 What is the main idea of paragraph 3?
   a. Jenny Currie is not typical of her generation.
   b. The majority of boomerang kids are college graduates.
   c. The rise of the Boomerang Generation is due to economic conditions.
   d. Canada has been particularly affected by the slow economy.

3 According to paragraph 3, which group had the highest wage increase between 1981 and 2011?
   a. Men between 25 and 34 years old
   b. Men between 45 and 54 years old
   c. Women between 25 and 34 years old
   d. Women between 45 and 54 years old

4 What advantage does Jenny have, according to paragraph 4?
   a. She can do her work from anywhere.
   b. She has unusually low student loan payments.
   c. She does not have to pay rent.
   d. She has very wealthy parents.

5 It can be inferred from the last paragraph that the author _____.
   a. was a boomerang kid himself once
   b. thinks boomerang kids are immature
   c. thinks parents should make boomerang kids move out
   d. has sympathy for boomerang kids

❷   Complete the sentences with information from the passage.

1 Besides Canada, three other countries with a Boomerang Generation mentioned in the passage
   are _____.

2 In 2011, the proportion of Canadians aged 20 to 29 living at home had risen to _____
   _____.

3 Jenny spends about one-fourth of her income on _____.

4 It has become hard for many young people to find _____.

Talk about the questions with a partner.

1 Many people go heavily into debt in order to pay for college. Do you think college is worth it? Why or why not?

2 If they don't want to move in with their parents, how else can young people deal with their financial problems?

CRITICAL THINKING

> ### Classifying Claims
>
> Arguments are a sequence of statements in which one statement (the conclusion) is supported by the others (the premises). Statements can generally be classified as either facts or opinions. A statement of fact tells something that is true about the world, whereas an expression of opinion tells what someone believes to be true. You can check statements of fact, but you must evaluate opinions, or **claims**, according to the support provided by the author and your own knowledge.
>
> Statements of opinion can be further categorized according to the kind of claim being made. Recognizing these can be helpful in analyzing arguments. Below are some types of claims:
>
> - **Prediction:** a claim that something will happen in the future, or as a result of something else
> - **Hypothesis:** a claim that is put forward for consideration, to be tested or investigated
> - **Causal explanation:** a claim about why something has happened or is as it is
> - **Recommendation:** a claim about what should be done in a given situation
> - **Allegation:** a claim that is made without complete proof, very often blaming or accusing someone
> - **Value judgment:** a claim that something is good or bad, right or wrong, desirable or undesirable, etc.
> - **Statement of principle:** a general claim expressing a basic truth, rule, or guideline

Read the excerpts from Reading 2. Then identify each underlined statement as F (fact), P (prediction), C (causal explanation), or V (value judgment).

1

(a.) _____ The main reason these grown children decide to go back home is financial. As in Jenny's case, most boomerang kids are well-educated and enthusiastic to live independently. However, the wages they receive are simply insufficient to support them. (b.) _____ According to Employment and Social Development Canada, between 1981 and 2011, "the proportion of young adults aged 20 to 29 who resided in their parental home rose fifteen percentage points from twenty-seven percent to forty-two percent."

2

(a.) _____ According to Statistics Canada, in 2007, the unemployment rate was at a 33-year low of six percent. In 2009, it rose to 8.6 percent. It has dropped a little in recent years; but as the newer generations hit the job market, (b.) _____ unemployment will very likely increase again in years to come. Couple that with high student loans to pay off, and (c.) _____ Jenny's move back home appears to be not only a wise financial move but a necessary one.

VOCABULARY REVIEW

Fill in the blanks with the correct words from the box. Change the form of the word if necessary.

restore	transition	accompany	eliminate
redefine	constrain	residence	assistance

1 Please provide addresses for both your _____ and your place of work.

2 Over the past century, the word *feminism* has been _____ by each new generation.

3 The ancient monument will be closed to the public while it is being _____.

4 The kinds of crops that can be grown in a certain area are _____ by the local climate.

5 Efforts to _____ diseases such as polio have been very successful.

6 The disabled and other passengers who need _____ may board first.

7 For first graders, the _____ to attending school full-time can be scary.

8 The illness is often _____ by nausea, fever, and fatigue.

 Go to page 191 of the Skills Handbook for the Writing Worksheet.

10 Different Ways of Friendship

Comparing male and female relationships with friends

How do male and female friendships differ?

Men kick friendship around like a football, but it doesn't seem to crack. Women treat it like glass, and it goes to pieces.

Anne Morrow Lindbergh

What you'll learn in this unit:

Reading 1 / Girls Feel More Anger When Friends Offend
Reading Skill: Summarizing

Reading 2 / Male and Female Friendships: Shoulder-to-Shoulder
Face-to-Face
Critical Thinking Skill: Recognizing Common Fallacies: Appeals to
Popularity or Tradition

Unit Project

Make Your Point
Express your opinion about the differences between male and female friendships

Before You Read

1 **Read the statements. Check (✔) whether you agree or disagree with each statement. Discuss your answers with a partner.**

	Strongly disagree	Disagree somewhat	Agree somewhat	Strongly agree
1. Male and female friendships are very different.				
2. Women's friendships are closer than men's.				
3. Men don't talk about their feelings with their male friends.				
4. Women fight with their friends more often than men do.				

2 **Think about the last time you had a fight with a friend. Answer the questions and discuss your answers with a partner.**

- What caused the disagreement?
- How did the disagreement make you feel?
- Did you resolve it? How?

Reading 1

VOCABULARY PREVIEW

Read the sentence. Circle the choice that is closest to the meaning of the AWL word in bold.

1 Both boys and girls struggle when serious **violations** of friendship occur.
   a. offenses   b. surprises   c. events

2 The children in the study were of various **ethnicities**.
   a. regions   b. social classes   c. races

3 Girls are more **communicative** about their emotions than boys are.
   a. confused   b. aware   c. open

4 Boys are less likely to seek **resolutions** to conflicts.
   a. answers   b. causes   c. feelings

5 The researchers **hypothesized** that girls get more upset when a friend offends them.
   a. argued   b. supposed   c. denied

6 It's harder for girls to cope **psychologically** when a friend lets them down.
   a. socially   b. mentally   c. easily

7 Feeling sad actually **intensifies** the desire to resolve the conflict.
   a. makes obvious   b. affects   c. makes stronger

8 We can use these **revelations** to help kids maintain their friendships.
   a. discoveries   b. theories   c. principles

READING PREVIEW

This passage is an online article about a study of children's friendships.

Do you think young girls and boys react differently when a friend hurts their feelings? If so, how? Discuss with a partner.

Track 19

Girls Feel More Anger When Friends Offend

by Steve Hartsoe
© 2011, Duke University. Used by permission.

C Predict what this passage will be about:

(1) How girls and boys react when friends hurt their feelings

(2) Why nice girls turn nasty when friends hurt their feelings

"Sugar and spice and everything nice; that's what little girls are made of," goes the old nursery rhyme[1]. But it turns out[2] that "everything nice" takes a back seat for girls when friends let them down.

Girls are just as likely as boys to verbally attack friends who have offended them.

In a Duke University study, researchers found that pre-teen girls may not be any better at friendships 5 than boys are, despite previous research suggesting otherwise. The findings suggest that when more serious **violations** of a friendship occur, girls struggle just as much as, and in some ways even more than, boys. The girls in this study were just as likely as boys 10 to report that they would seek revenge[3] against an offending friend, verbally attack the friend, and threaten to end the friendship when their expectations were violated, such as telling one of their secrets to other children. The girls also reported they were more bothered by the transgressions[4], felt more anger and sadness, and were more likely to think the offense meant their friend did not care 15 about them or was trying to control them.

Q When friendship expectations are violated, who is more likely to seek revenge , boys or girls?

The study was co-authored by Julie Paquette MacEvoy, a former Duke Ph.D. student who is now an assistant professor at Boston College's Lynch School of Education, and Steven Asher, a professor in Duke's Department of Psychology and Neuroscience. MacEvoy and Asher surveyed 267 fourth- and fifth-grade children of diverse **ethnicities**: 49.3 percent 20 Caucasian, 26.6 percent Latino, 21.5 percent African-American, and 2.6 percent "other."

The children heard sixteen stories in which they were asked to imagine that a friend had violated a core expectation of friendship. One of these stories included a friend failing to hold up responsibilities in a joint school project, resulting in a bad grade for both friends. Another involved a friend failing to show concern about another friend's sick pet, saying, 25 "It's no big deal, it's just a pet." For each story, the 9- to 11-year-olds were asked how they would feel if the incident really happened to them. They were also asked how they would interpret the friend's behavior, what they would do, and how much the incident would bother them.

Q Underline two hypothetical situations used in the study.

---

[1] **nursery rhyme** *n.* a poem or song for children
[2] **turn out** *phrasal v.* to result in a certain way; to become clear or known

[3] **revenge** *n.* the act of hurting someone because that person hurt you
[4] **transgression** *n.* a violation

³⁰ "Previous research suggests that girls may hold their friends to a higher standard than boys do. This led us to think that girls might have an especially hard time coping[5] if one of their friends does something to disappoint them," MacEvoy said. Other studies have suggested that girls are better at friendships than boys are because girls are more emotionally **communicative** in their friendships, girls help their friends more, and girls
³⁵ more readily seek **resolutions** to conflicts with their friends. Yet, previous studies also found that boys' friendships last just as long as those of girls, that boys are just as satisfied with their friendships as girls are, and that boys are no lonelier than girls.

Q Underline three similarities between boys and girls.

The researchers **hypothesized** that there was a good explanation for this paradox[6]: girls have a particularly difficult time coping **psychologically** when a friend disappoints them.
⁴⁰ "Our finding that girls would be just as vengeful[7] and aggressive toward their friends as boys would is particularly interesting because past research has consistently shown boys to react more negatively following minor conflicts with friends, such as an argument about which game to play next," Asher said. "It appears that friendship transgressions and conflicts of interest may push different buttons for boys and girls."

⁴⁵ The study found that anger and sadness played significant roles in how boys and girls reacted to offending friends. For both genders, the more strongly they felt a friend had devalued[8] them or was trying to control them, the more anger and
⁵⁰ sadness they felt. Further, the angrier they felt, the less likely they were to want to fix the relationship. But in both genders, feelings of sadness actually **intensified** the desire for reconciliation[9]: the more sadness the children reported feeling, the

After a fight, feeling sad motivates both boys and girls to repair the friendship.

⁵⁵ more anxious they were to solve the problem and maintain the friendship. Sadness, the authors said, can sometimes function like "social glue" that holds relationships together.

Q What effect does anger have on both boys and girls? Underline the information.

These **revelations** can provide guidance on helping children maintain their friendships in a healthy way. This is especially true for girls when a friend is unreliable, doesn't provide emotional support or help, or betrays them, the researchers said. "When we try to help
⁶⁰ children who are struggling in their friendships, we may need to focus on somewhat different issues for boys versus girls," MacEvoy said. "For girls, it may be critical to help them learn how to cope better when a friend lets them down."

---

⁵ **cope** *v.* to deal with; to manage
⁶ **paradox** *n.* a situation in which two things that seem to be opposites are both true
⁷ **vengeful** *adj.* feeling or showing a desire for revenge

⁸ **devalue** *v.* to make something or someone seem less valuable or important
⁹ **reconciliation** *n.* the act of becoming friendly again after an argument or disagreement

MAPPING IDEAS

 Comprehension

Organize the ideas from Reading 1. Review the passage and fill in the graphic organizer below.

How girls react when friends offend

How study was done:
- A group of kids aged [1] _____ from different ethnic groups
- Asked to imagine a friend did something to hurt them
- Described what they would do and how they would feel

Results of study:
- Boys and girls equally likely to attack, try to get revenge
- Girls angrier and [2] _____ than boys
- For both, sadness made them want to [3] _____

Previous research:
- Girls hold friends to higher standards, communicate and help more, and try to [4] _____
- Boys' friendships just as long and satisfying as girls'

Conclusions:
- Harder for girls to deal with [5] _____
- New findings can be used to help kids maintain friendships

 Before you go on, boost your reading skills. Go to page 193 of the Skills Handbook.

FOCUS ON CONTENT

Comprehension

① Circle the main idea of the passage. For each of the other sentences, check the reason it is not the main idea.

1 Studies show various differences in the friendships of boys and girls.

☐ too general   ☐ too specific   ☐ not in passage   ☐ inaccurate

2 Surprising new research suggests girls find it more difficult than boys to cope with being disappointed by a friend.

☐ too general   ☐ too specific   ☐ not in passage   ☐ inaccurate

3 A new study suggests that, in general, girls are better at maintaining friendships than boys are.

☐ too general   ☐ too specific   ☐ not in passage   ☐ inaccurate

4 For both boys and girls, the angrier they are at a friend, the more likely they are to give up on the friendship.

☐ too general   ☐ too specific   ☐ not in passage   ☐ inaccurate

2 **Choose the best answer.**

1 According to paragraph 2, in response to a serious friendship violation, girls were more likely than boys to _____.

   a. think the friend was trying to control them

   b. want revenge against the friend

   c. confront the friend verbally

   d. say they might end their relationship with the friend

2 What is the topic of paragraph 7?

   a. Gender differences in the way people fix friendships

   b. Reasons boys experience less anger at friendship violations

   c. The importance of anger and sadness for both genders in friendship violations

   d. Gender differences in responding to sadness

3 **Mark each statement as true (T) or false (F) according to the passage.**

_____ **1** In the study, children were asked about past experiences with friends who let them down.

_____ **2** The majority of children in the study were Caucasian.

_____ **3** Girls responded to friendship transgressions as aggressively as boys did.

_____ **4** Research found that boys experience more loneliness than girls.

_____ **5** Studies suggest that conflicts of interest affect boys more negatively than girls.

THINK AND DISCUSS

1 **Read the excerpt from the reading passage.**

Girls Feel More Anger When Friends Offend

"When we try to help children who are struggling in their friendships, we may need to focus on somewhat different issues for boys versus girls," MacEvoy said. "For girls, it may be critical to help them learn how to cope better when a friend lets them down."

Discuss the following questions with a partner.

• What should be the focus when helping boys who are struggling in their friendships?

• Do you think the gender differences found in research on kids are true for adults as well?

❷ **Imagine you found out that one of your best friends had made an unkind joke about you to others. Write a brief answer to the questions.**

- How would you feel?

- What would you do about it, if anything?

- Do you think most people of the opposite sex would give answers different from yours?

_____

_____

_____

_____

_____

_____

VOCABULARY REVIEW

Fill in the blanks with the correct words from the box. Change the form of the word if necessary.

resolution	psychologically	intensify	violation
communicative	hypothesize	revelation	ethnicity

1 As I entered the kitchen, the delicious smell of baking _____ my hunger.

2 In his new book, the author _____ that the world's population will begin decreasing by 2050.

3 Traveling for a long time is exhausting, both physically and _____.

4 It is not always possible to guess a person's _____ by just looking at him or her.

5 The fascinating _____ in the former president's biography made the book a bestseller.

6 Because it puts people's lives at risk, drinking and driving is a serious _____.

7 Let's hope that a(n) _____ can be reached so that the two nations do not go to war.

8 Police tried to question the suspect, but he was not very _____.

VOCABULARY PREVIEW

Match each AWL word in bold with its meaning from the box.

a. naturally; without thinking	b. in a large, or major, way
c. for a long time; customarily	d. an event causing great and sudden damage and suffering
e. increased or built up over time	f. the act of leaving or taking away support
g. the state of being complicated	h. a limit or boundary

_____ **1** Between female friends, loss of trust is a **catastrophe**, both socially and psychologically.

_____ **2** Common ideas about men and women do not express the **complexities** of individuals.

_____ **3** Males often form friendships within the **parameters** of shared activities.

_____ **4** Among female friends, **abandonment** is the worst crime.

_____ **5** Boys **automatically** build friendships based on playing games together.

_____ **6** **Traditionally**, girls and women have been viewed as more emotional.

_____ **7** Female bonding is **significantly** different from male bonding.

_____ **8** Women build friendship based on the **accumulated** experiences they share.

READING PREVIEW

This essay compares and contrasts women's friendships and men's friendships.

What do women usually do together as they get to know a new friend? What about men? Discuss with a partner.

Male and Female Friendships: Shoulder-to-Shoulder vs. Face-to-Face

Track 20

by Kelly Shepherd / Language Cradle Consulting

Men and women think and feel differently about a myriad[1] of subjects, and this includes the friendships they have. **Traditionally**, females are seen as being more driven by their feelings, and males are seen as more oriented toward action. Movies and books commonly depict female friendships as centered on sharing emotions, seeking and giving advice, and providing empathy[2]. Their friendships are created and maintained 5 around those activities. Men, however, are put into roles as action figures: they go out and conquer enemies and become heroes with a friend beside them, much like Batman and Robin.

These stories perpetuate[3] stereotypes surrounding how men and women differ, and stereotypes, of course, never express the full **complexity** of real women and men. 10 However, it can't be denied that they have some basis in reality.

Men's friendships are usually based on sports and other "shoulder-to-shoulder" activities.

C Underline the appeal to authority in this paragraph.

From an early age, male friendships are typically built around sports and games, as boys generally love competing against one another. Males seem to **automatically** form friendships through shared activities rather than through shared feelings. In one survey of Americans, eighty percent of men said they participated in sports with their friends. Not a single woman gave that answer. "Men do not easily make revelations of strong emotional responses," Dr. Roger Gould, a psychiatrist, told *Atlantic Monthly*. But doing things together provides an experience of shared accomplishment and recognition. Boys and men learn to support one another within these **parameters**, and this builds bonds between them. 15

20

To use terms coined by psychologist Paul Wright, while men have "shoulder-to-shoulder" friendships, women have "face-to-face" ones. Females also enjoy sharing common 25 experiences; however, their bonding methods are **significantly** different from those of males. It is more important for females to communicate verbally with one another. Women's studies and education scholar Lyn Mikel Brown asserts that a female's friendships are a "psychological safety net." Women share issues of work, family, and relationships with their friends as common ground for exploring ways to handle tough situations. These 30 **accumulated** experiences are important factors within female friendships, helping them get through the problems they face.

Q List the similarity and difference between men and women in forming friendships.

[1] **myriad** *n.* a very large number
[2] **empathy** *n.* shared emotion based on shared or similar experiences
[3] **perpetuate** *v.* to cause to continue

Women's friendships tend to form and grow through "face-to-face" experiences.

Bonding is a high priority for both males and females. Yet females seem to place more importance on the loyalty and trust these bonds create than do males. This may be because women develop such intense bonds in their friendships that, when a disagreement comes up, it could have a deeper effect on their lives than it would on men's lives. A loss of trust between female friends is not a matter of a simple disagreement, but more like a psychological and social **catastrophe**.

This is skillfully portrayed in the 2004 movie *Mean Girls*, in which the main character, a girl named Cady, is a newcomer at her high school. She quickly makes friends with the outsider Janis, who warns Cady to stay away from a group of popular but mean girls that have bullied her for years. However, Cady is gradually drawn into the mean girls' social circle and ultimately snubs[4] Janis, who is deeply hurt and angry. The movie earned over $100 million worldwide, so obviously its depiction of female friendships is believable. It gives us a realistic glimpse[5] into female relationships, in which trust is everything, and betrayal and **abandonment** are the worst possible crimes.

In an article titled "The Complicated Business of Female Friendships," the author Elizabeth Gilbert suggests that the ending of female friendships can be "just as painful as any severed[6] romantic relationship." Female friendships are difficult to replace because women invest so much in their friendships. This does not mean that males view the friendships they have as being any less important than females do; the difference is in how they approach the problems that arise within those friendships.

On the website artofmanliness.com, a post titled "The History and Nature of Man Friendship" describes the tactics[7] males use when irritated by one another. "When a guy is bothered by something that his friend is doing, he simply tells his friend; they discuss it, sometimes heatedly[8], and then move on." Males don't see a point in brooding[9] over something their friend said or did. They also don't impose their views on their friends if they disagree about something. Males, it seems, would rather get to the bottom of[10] the issue. If they don't see eye to eye, they don't have a problem walking away from the friendship.

To sum up, books and movies aren't entirely wrong: men's and women's friendships are distinct from one another. But in both sexes, they bind people together through shared experiences and accomplishments. Friendships are among our most meaningful relationships, carrying both women and men through their lives in an enriching way.

Q What do men do when a friend's action bothers them? Underline the information.

C Underline the conclusion of this passage.

---

[4] **snub** *v.* to ignore in an insulting way

[5] **glimpse** *n.* a look

[6] **severed** *adj.* cut off; ended

[7] **tactic** *n.* an action meant to achieve a goal

[8] **heatedly** *adv.* with excited or angry feelings

[9] **brood** *v.* to think anxiously or sadly

[10] **get to the bottom of (something)** *idiom* to find an explanation for; to discover the truth about

FOCUS ON CONTENT

❶ Choose the best answer.

○ Comprehension

1 The author thinks that fictional portrayals of male and female friendships are _____.
  a. completely different from reality
  b. accurate about women but not about men
  c. based on outdated facts and customs
  d. overly simple but partly true

2 What is the main idea of paragraph 3?
  a. Boys' friendships are similar to men's.
  b. Sports are more important to men than to women.
  c. Male bonding centers on shared activities.
  d. Both boys and men enjoy competition.

3 Why does the author discuss the movie *Mean Girls*?
  a. To illustrate a point about how much women value trust
  b. To give an example of a wrong depiction of female friendship
  c. To help explain why women's friendships have more conflict
  d. To argue that female friends are more likely to betray each other

4 What can be inferred from paragraph 7?
  a. A man and woman who were romantically involved cannot be friends anymore.
  b. Men tend to be less deeply affected by the loss of a friendship.
  c. When women lose a female friendship, they do not try to replace it.
  d. Women find it harder to have both close friends and a romantic relationship.

5 Which of the following is true, according to paragraph 8?
  a. When men are irritated with a friend, they usually don't say anything.
  b. Men usually insist that their friends agree with them.
  c. Men are quite likely to brood over a conflict with a friend.
  d. It's fairly easy for a man to end a friendship.

❷ Check the statements that are true according to the passage. Correct the false statements.

1 ☐ In an American survey, no women said they played sports with their friends.

_____

2 ☐ A psychologist first described men's friendships as "shoulder-to-shoulder."

_____

3 ☐ Bonding is not as important for men as it is for women.

_____

4 ☐ *Mean Girls* presents female friendships realistically.

_____

IDEAS IN ACTION

Talk about the questions with a partner.

1 What is a movie or book that you think presents male or female friendship in a believable way?

2 Think about your own experiences with (male or female) friendship. Are they similar to the descriptions in the reading?

CRITICAL THINKING

Recognizing Common Fallacies: Appeal to Popularity or Tradition

It is common for people to think that if something is liked or believed by many people, then it must be valid, true, or good. Writers may take advantage of this by using an **appeal to popularity**, a common fallacy in which the popularity of an idea or belief is presented as evidence in favor of it. The form of this type of argument is as follows: *A lot of people like/do/believe X. Therefore, X must be good/correct.*

For example:

> Nearly half of all Americans believe that ghosts exist. That's over 150 million people. Surely, they are not all wrong.

This is a fallacy because large numbers of people can be wrong.

People also tend to believe older, traditional ideas more easily than new ones. Thus, a related fallacy is the **appeal to tradition**. This is similar to the appeal to popularity, only it is about the past. It usually takes this form: *People have liked/done/believed X for a long time. Therefore, X must be good/correct.*

For example:

> Traditional Chinese medicine is thousands of years old, much older than Western medicine. It must be superior.

---

1 **Read the excerpt from Reading 2. Underline the appeal to popularity.**

> This is skillfully portrayed in the 2004 movie *Mean Girls*, in which the main character, a girl named Cady, is a newcomer at her high school. She quickly makes friends with the outsider Janis, who warns Cady to stay away from a group of popular but mean girls that have bullied her for years. However, Cady is gradually drawn into the mean girls' social circle and ultimately snubs Janis, who is deeply hurt and angry. The movie earned over $100 million worldwide, so obviously its depiction of female friendships is believable. It gives us a realistic glimpse into female relationships, in which trust is everything, and betrayal and abandonment are the worst possible crimes.

② **Read the appeal to tradition. Write the conclusion. Explain why it is a fallacy.**

> Recently, it became possible to get a college degree online. But classes have been taught in person since the first university was founded in the Middle Ages. _____
> _____.

This is a fallacy because _____

_____.

VOCABULARY REVIEW

Fill in the blanks with the correct words from the box. Change the form of the word if necessary.

automatically	accumulated	abandonment	traditionally
complexity	catastrophe	significantly	parameter

1 Dr. Henson was pleased to see that the patient's condition had _____ improved.

2 The spread of the cane toad throughout Australia has been an ecological _____ for the country.

3 If you join our gym, you don't have to worry about paying your fee; it will be _____ charged to your credit card every month.

4 I had to leave my dog behind when I moved abroad, and I still feel guilty about that act of _____.

5 Planning for the project must stay within the _____ of the budget and the deadline.

6 The British and the French have _____ been both friends and rivals.

7 Due to the _____ of the tax system, many people have to hire professionals to figure out what they owe.

8 By the end of his life, the famous investor's _____ wealth amounted to over $1 billion.

Go to page 194 of the Skills Handbook for the Writing Worksheet.

11

Are You Being Watched?

The value of privacy in the modern world

Think About It

Do you feel safe knowing that companies and other organizations collect information about you?

You have to fight for your privacy or you lose it.

Eric Schmidt

What you'll learn in this unit:	Reading 1 / **How Tracking Customers In-store Will Soon Be the Norm** **Reading Skill:** Facts and Opinions
	Reading 2 / **Governmental Privacy Protections: The Cases of Germany and Malaysia** **Critical Thinking Skill:** Recognizing Common Fallacies: *Ad Hominem*, Straw Man, Slippery Slope

Unit Project	**Make Your Point** Express your opinion about organizations collecting people's private information

Before You Read

❶ Check (✔) which information you would share publicly and which you would not. Discuss your answers with a partner.

	Share with anyone	Share only with friends and family	Share only with friends	Share with no one
1. Your real name (first and last names)				
2. Your age				
3. Your phone number				
4. Your address				
5. Your favorite brands				
6. Where you like to shop				
7. What you eat				
8. Your friends' names				
9. The websites you visit				
10. How much money you make				

❷ Mark the statements as Y (yes) or N (no). Then discuss with a partner why you mind or don't mind your privacy being invaded in these ways.

1 Are you a private person? _____

2 Do your parents or other family members invade your privacy? _____

3 Do you mind if security cameras record you in public places? _____

4 Do social media sites like Facebook violate your privacy? _____

5 Do you read privacy agreements before you use online services? _____

VOCABULARY PREVIEW

Match each AWL word in bold with its meaning from the box.

a. a committee	b. hesitant and unwilling
c. to put into action	d. combined
e. to gather	f. a set of rules
g. new	h. permission

_____ **1** Companies will be able to **implement** the system at their stores for free.

_____ **2** Now there is no reason for **reluctant** businesses not to use it.

_____ **3** A **code** of conduct was launched to control how companies use customer information.

_____ **4** Companies are required to get customers' **consent** before they use any private information

_____ **5** A government **commission** praised the company for being respectful of consumers' privacy.

_____ **6** Data is **compiled** to determine ways to make advertising personal.

_____ **7** At this time, the company is only able to give **aggregate** information.

_____ **8** The obvious goal of this **emerging** technology is to identify individual customers.

READING PREVIEW

This passage is an article about how companies are using new technologies to monitor consumers' behaviors to collect marketing information.

Why do you think companies might want information about where you go, what you do, and what you buy? Think of a few ideas and share them with a partner.

How Tracking Customers In-store Will Soon Be the Norm

Track 21

by Siraj Datoo
© 2014, Guardian News and Media Limited. Used by permission.

At the Fairson's department store, managers can measure the number of people who walk past the store and the number who come through the front door. Also, this information includes whether or not these people come in immediately or are convinced to do so by the shop front.

Once shoppers are inside the store, managers can find out how many of them walk up 5 to the second floor and compare that with the number of people who took the journey to the second floor last week. If more people have gone up this week, managers will probably conclude that the marketing banners put up toward the beginning of the week are working.

In this scenario, Fairson's is imaginary. But this technology is very real. Euclid, a California- 10 based analytics[1] company, is hoping to gain wider acceptance of tracking technology by offering its Euclid Express for free to all retailers[2]. This means that, at no cost, stores will be able to **implement** an analytics package to receive information that could help guide their marketing.

Why is Euclid offering its services at no cost to clients? One reason is competition. 15 Euclid's is currently the only offline customer analytics platform that is available for free. This provides the company with a strong competitive advantage over rivals such as ShopperTrak and Prism Skylabs. Moreover, Euclid wants to lower the barriers[3] to entry so there is no longer any reason for **reluctant** businesses not to implement this technology.

Stores can collect information through customers' smart phones.

Late in 2012, Euclid released its next product, called 20 Euclid Zero. Eliminating the need for companies to install sensors[4] in their stores, Euclid Zero connects retailers to a cloud-based analytics service using Wi-Fi. Businesses then collect information about customer behavior by monitoring the media access code (MAC) in every smart 25 phone that enters the store.

Euclid Zero has received a lot of criticism from consumers concerned about their privacy being violated[5]. But Euclid assures that the MAC data is scrambled[6], which means that no personally identifiable information is collected. Second, they point to the fact that Euclid is a part of the group that launched the Mobile Location Analytics **code** of conduct[7]. These 30 sets of rules require companies to receive customers' **consent** before they can collect any

Q What is Euclid's strategy for getting more retailers to use its technology? Underline it.

Q Euclid gives three responses to concerns about its technology. What are they? Underline them.

---

[1] **analytics** *n.* the logical analysis of data and statistics
[2] **retailer** *n.* a person or business that sells goods directly to the public
[3] **barrier** *n.* phrase to reduce something that is blocking or preventing a process

[4] **sensor** *n.* a device that detects and responds to certain changes in the environment
[5] **violate** *v.* to not respect someone's right to something
[6] **scramble** *v.* to mix up a signal or message so that it cannot be understood
[7] **conduct** *n.* the way a person acts; behavior

personal information. Euclid also helped found a central opt-out[8] site for consumers. This site was praised by the Federal Trade **Commission** for "recognising consumer concerns about invisible tracking in retail spaces and taking a positive step forward in developing a code of conduct."

But it's worth noting that the code of conduct most likely was signed following complaints from angry customers when they found out that they were being monitored. For instance, American department store Nordstrom put up a sign in May 2013 that announced it had been using the technology for months. Subsequently, it received a number of complaints made directly to its store and also on social media.

C What inference does the author make about the reason why the code of conduct was created?

The potential for the technology also means that it could upset many. "I would think permission would need to be given to use something that belongs to someone else. Even if it is just a signal," one consumer posted on Facebook.

Another example is that of a marketing startup company named Renew in Britain. It tracked pedestrians in the City of London through their smart phones using devices hidden in recycling bins. Renew claimed that people could opt out if they so desire, but privacy supporters questioned the idea of people opting out of something they didn't know was taking place.

Renew planned on using the data it was **compiling** to provide shoppers with personalised advertising on their digital screens. "Why not Pret?" is a message that might be displayed to a regular visitor of Starbucks, the main competitor of café Pret a Manger. Over time, Renew could also tell whether consumers have altered their habits.

But Renew's CEO was adamant[9] that this was not personal information. "As long as we don't add a name and home address, it's legal," he said.

This adds a new element[10] to the conversation. As it stands, Euclid provides only **aggregate** information. But there is potential for more personalised marketing. For instance, a coffee drinker visiting a store might see a message informing him or her of a coffee shop on the second floor. Although the company would not know whom exactly it was marketing to, it would still understand the person's shopping habits.

Q What example of personalised marketing does the author give in this paragraph?

Emma Carr, a senior director at Big Brother Watch, believes that this technology ignores customers' privacy. "This is a clear example of profit trumping[11] privacy," she said. "The use of surveillance technology by shops in order to provide a better or more personalised service seems totally disproportionate[12]."

Carr also stressed the importance of consumer awareness. She said that while the **emerging** technology was still developing, there was an obvious goal in mind to identify individuals. Companies like Euclid won't stop at general information like the length of time that customers spend in stores. The long game is about identifying individuals, and this technology is very close to enabling Euclid to do that.

"It is not only essential that customers are fully informed if they are being monitored, but that they also have real choice of service and on what terms it is offered."

This type of personalised *Minority Report*-style marketing has sparked a new debate: Is your MAC your personal information?

---

[8] **opt-out** *n.* a decision not to participate

[9] **adamant** *adj.* determined not to change one's decision or opinion

[10] **element** *n.* a basic part of something

[11] **trump** *v.* to surpass or outdo

[12] **disproportionate** *adj.* out of proportion, as in quantity or appearance; unbalanced

MAPPING IDEAS

Organize the ideas from Reading 1. Review the passage and fill in the graphic organizer below.

Customer tracking systems

System	• Euclid Express offered [1] _____ to help guide marketing • Euclid Zero connects retailers to [2] _____ to monitor customers' smartphones	• Renew tracked people in London using [6] _____ to provide personalized advertising
Fears	• Customers worry their [3] _____ and that their MAC data is in danger	• Customers could opt-out, but they [7] _____
Justification	• Euclid says MAC data is [4] _____ • Also formed a [5] _____ that requires users' consent to collect info	• No [8] _____ included, so customers' identities remain private

R W Before you go on, boost your reading skills. Go to page 195 of the Skills Handbook.

FOCUS ON CONTENT

Comprehension

1 **Circle the main idea of the passage. For each of the other sentences, check the reason it is not the main idea.**

1 Technology companies are losing business clients because their technologies are intruding on customers' privacy.

☐ too general   ☐ too specific   ☐ not in passage   ☐ inaccurate

2 Stores are required to inform customers about the personal data collection technologies that they are using.

☐ too general   ☐ too specific   ☐ not in passage   ☐ inaccurate

3 All social media users should be aware of Facebook's privacy policy.

☐ too general   ☐ too specific   ☐ not in passage   ☐ inaccurate

4 New technologies that are being used by companies for marketing research raise privacy concerns.

☐ too general   ☐ too specific   ☐ not in passage   ☐ inaccurate

2 **Mark each statement as true (T) or false (F) according to the passage.**

_____ **1** Euclid's free offer gives the company an advantage over its competitors.

_____ **2** Media access codes are transmitted by smart phones and can be used for collecting personal information.

_____ **3** The Federal Trade Commission disagrees with the methods that Euclid uses to protect consumer privacy.

_____ **4** The code of conduct Euclid helped produce was probably a response to customer complaints about being watched.

3 **Choose the best answer.**

1 All of the following are ways that Euclid protects consumers' privacy EXCEPT:

a. They operate a website where consumers can opt out of being monitored

b. They created a privacy code of consumers can opt out follow

c. They scramble the personal information that their technology collects

d. They report retailers that do not protect people's personal information

2 According to the reading passage, which statement would Emily Carr agree with?

a. Personalized marketing is a trend that retailers and consumers should embrace.

b. Companies will move away from collecting only general information to data that identifies people.

c. People can trust the government to make sure companies do not invade their privacy.

d. All advertisements should be clearly marked and displayed where customers can see them.

THINK AND DISCUSS

1 **Read the excerpt from the reading passage.**

How Tracking Customers In-store Will Soon Be the Norm

For instance, American department store Nordstrom put up a sign in May 2013 that announced it had been using the technology for months. Subsequently, it received a number of complaints made directly to its store and also on social media.

Discuss the following questions with a partner.

- How would you feel if a store you shopped at regularly had been monitoring your shopping behavior without your knowing?
- How would you respond in this situation?

❷ The passage focuses on how stores and companies invade people's privacy. Are there other situations in which you have had your privacy invaded? How, where, and by whom was your privacy violated? Write a short response.

On the Internet

By parents or friends

At school

_____

_____

_____

VOCABULARY REVIEW

❶ **Match each word to its definition.**

1 aggregate (adj.) •   • **a** a set of laws or rules

2 code (n.) •   • **b** an official group of people chosen to perform a certain task

3 commission (n.) •   • **c** added up or considered together

4 compile (v.) •   • **d** to put into action; to make use of

5 consent (n.) •   • **e** approval or permission of another's plan or action

6 emerging (adj.) •   • **f** hesitant and unwilling to do something

7 reluctant (adj.) •   • **g** coming into existence; developing

8 implement (v.) •   • **h** to bring together; to collect

❷ **Fill in the blanks with the correct words from above. Change the form of the word if necessary.**

1 The woman claims that the store used her picture in their ad without her _____.

2 A(n) _____ problem is addiction to smart phones.

3 Businesses _____ information about what consumers do online to help them make advertising decisions.

4 The government put together a(n) _____ to draft rules for how companies can collect and use customer data.

5 Most people are _____ to give personal information to strangers, particularly over the phone.

Reading 2

VOCABULARY PREVIEW

Read the sentence. Circle the choice that is closest to the meaning of the AWL word in bold.

1 People have claimed to have been **terminated** from their jobs after putting inappropriate content on the Internet.

a. blocked

b. promoted

c. fired

2 The problem of privacy invasion has **compounded** in the past few decades.

a. endured

b. lessened

c. intensified

3 **Hypothetically**, the government would be watching citizens all the time.

a. theoretically

b. incorrectly

c. adequately

4 The law clearly states that the privacy of personal information is **inviolable**.

a. strong

b. protected

c. secret

5 There was no **coherent** law about privacy protection until only a few years ago.

a. strict

b. shifting

c. consistent

6 The act contains **clauses** that allow the police to monitor people's phone calls and emails.

a. suggestions

b. statements

c. documents

7 Germany's **constitution** provides for privacy protection.

a. high court

b. mass media

c. set of laws

8 Governments **suspend** some privacy rights for national security reason.

a. waive

b. allow

c. prohibit

READING PREVIEW

This passage is about privacy protection laws. The author discusses how countries take different approaches to protecting their citizens' privacy.

Do you think it is OK for governments to listen to people's phone calls and read their emails? If yes, in what situations? If no, why not? Make a list of reasons and share it with a partner.

Track 22

Governmental Privacy Protections: The Cases of Germany and Malaysia

by Jon Maes / Language Cradle Consulting

Are there any Internet searches you have done that you would not want anyone to know about? Well, you might be surprised to learn that most search engines store search terms and other identifying information for every search you make. In fact, there is probably a lot more of your personal data being stored online than you realize, and that can be a scary thought.

Even more disturbing[1] is how online activities have adversely impacted some people's lives. For instance, searching for information about a terrorist group for a school project has landed some students on government watch lists. Then, there are insurance companies that have used customers' searches about illnesses and other health conditions to raise those people's insurance rates or deny them coverage. There are also stories about people claiming that they were wrongfully **terminated** from their jobs because of photos posted on social media sites.

Q What is governments' reason for taking away some privacy rights from citizens?

Social media activities can cost people their jobs.

Privacy concerns have been **compounded** in recent years because of several global threats. One is the rise in cybercrime following the spread of the Internet and information technologies. Another is the perceived increase in terrorist attacks. These issues have brought individuals' privacy rights into conflict with governments' responsibility to protect their citizens from harm. Governments use these dangers to **suspend** certain privacy rights in order to defend against such threats and maintain national security. The government's justification is that criminal actions are a serious problem that must be dealt with. In addition, governments point out that federal agencies have the best resources for defending against these threats. Therefore, citizens should trust the government with their personal information for their own protection.

On the other hand, there are concerns that governments have gone too far with mass surveillance, and in the process have violated people's rights to privacy. For example, some say the US government has gone beyond minimal information gathering to actually listening in on people's phone calls and reading their private email. They even argue that citizens should not give up any amount of privacy. Otherwise, the government would take away more and more privacy rights until there are none left. **Hypothetically**, this would create a world in which governments spy[2] on their citizens' every move.

Regardless of what the future holds, the world is currently split between countries that seek to safeguard[3] privacy and those that engage in mass surveillance. Germany and Malaysia are two examples of this divide.

---

[1] **disturbing** *adj.* causing a person to be upset or troubled

[2] **spy on** *phrasal v.* to secretly watch or collect information on someone or something

[3] **safeguard** *v.* to keep safe; to protect

Germany is recognized as one of the countries with the strictest privacy protections in Europe. Its **constitution** clearly states that the privacy of citizens' letters, online posts, and telecommunications[4] are **inviolable**. Germany is also home to the world's first data protection law. Originally passed in the state of Hesse in 1970, the legislation became a national act in 1977. Since then, the courts have time and again ruled in favor of protecting German citizens' right to privacy. This includes the decision in February 2008 that the government could not conduct secret online searches of private computers.

Q How does the author describe Germany compared to other countries in Europe regarding privacy protection laws?

Germany even extends the protection of its citizens' privacy beyond its borders. In 2010, a government official in Hamburg led an investigation into Facebook's Friend Finder application. He made a case against the application's use of people's email and mobile phone contacts to locate their friends, arguing that it infringes[5] on the privacy of people who do not use the social networking site. The inquiry pressured Facebook to make the application less intrusive[6]. Users now have more control over the contacts that are imported by Facebook. The site also has to ask users before sending out any friend invitations or notifications[7].

In contrast, Malaysia does not specify in its constitution that citizens have the right to privacy. It also did not have any **coherent** policy against privacy violations until the Personal Data Protection Act (PDPA) of 2010. However, there continues to be criticism of the PDPA, a major point of contention[8] being that it does not apply to federal or state agencies. The act still allows government officials to collect personal data including background, education, and health records. Also, government agents are not required to inform the person who is being monitored. As such, critics say that nothing has changed and that supporters of the PDPA have no concern for protecting privacy.

Q The author mentions two criticisms of Malaysia's Personal Data Protection Act. What are they? Underline them.

Moreover, the Malaysian government passed the Security Offences[9] (Special Measures) Act in 2012. The act contains **clauses** that give police the power to intercept[10] private communications without needing permission from a court. Police can also search any person's house and make arrests if they believe there is a national security threat. The concern is that they will abuse this power by targeting people who have different political opinions than the ruling government. The end result would be the invasion of people's privacy and the loss of personal freedoms.

The examples of Germany and Malaysia demonstrate clear differences in the approaches that countries take with regard to the privacy of their citizens. This indicates that the situation is complex and that personal information is less protected than before. Even when organizations claim the best intentions, citizens should still be mindful of who is watching their online activities. They should also be aware of how their personal information is being used because, in the end, each individual is the first line of defense against privacy violations.

---

4 **telecommunication** *n.* a message sent by one of the technologies for communicating over long distances

5 **infringe** *v.* to violate, break, or go beyond established limits

6 **intrusive** *adj.* bothersome and unwelcome

7 **notification** *n.* an act or instance that gives news, warning, or a sign of something

8 **contention** *n.* argument or disagreement

9 **offense** *n.* an act of breaking a law, disobeying a rule, or doing something wrong

10 **intercept** *v.* to stop or take hold of; to interrupt the movement or progress of something

FOCUS ON CONTENT

Comprehension

① Choose the best answer.

1 What is the main point of the passage?
   a. People can protect themselves from privacy invasions.
   b. People should give up some privacy rights for national security reasons.
   c. Privacy protection policies vary between countries.
   d. There should be fewer restrictions on Internet usage.

2 What is true about Germany with regard to privacy protection?
   a. It started the movement to provide for privacy protection in constitution.
   b. It is the first country to have established a data protection law.
   c. It has the most privacy protection court cases of any nation.
   d. It is the only country to have investigated Facebook for invasion of privacy.

3 Which of the following is NOT an act that the Malaysian government has authority to do?
   a. Search the house of any person whom it believes is a threat to national security
   b. Monitor a person without being required by law to inform that person about it
   c. Conduct surveillance of private communications without requesting permission from a judge
   d. Set up hidden security cameras in the houses of political opponents

4 What was the result of the Hamburg official's investigation of Facebook?
   a. Facebook changed its privacy policies to be less intrusive.
   b. The court case is still pending with no judicial decision yet.
   c. Other countries started their own investigations of Facebook.
   d. The CEO of Facebook was forced to resign from the company.

5 According to the passage, what has caused an increase in privacy issues? Choose two.
   a. Health-care concerns   b. Terrorism
   c. Social media   d. Cybercrime

② Match the years to the events.

1 1970 ____   **2** 1977 ____   **3** 2008 ____   **4** 2010 ____   **5** 2012 ____

a. A German court ruled against secret online searches of computers.	b. The German state of Hesse passed the data protection legislation.	c. The Security Offences (Special Measures) Act became law in Malaysia.

d. The Malaysian government passed the Personal Data Protection Act.	e. Data protection law was passed by the national government in Germany.

IDEAS IN ACTION

Talk about the questions with a partner.

1 Which government's approach to privacy protection do you agree with? Why?

2 What do you think the world would be like if there were no privacy?

CRITICAL THINKING

Recognizing Common Fallacies: *Ad Hominem*, Straw Man, Slippery Slope

There are certain kinds of arguments that are convincing but fallacious. Here are three common ones:

(1) **Ad hominem** is a kind of argument that focuses on attacking a person's reputation or background rather than his or her ideas on their own merit. For example:

> Robert is against the new shopping center. How could we possibly accept the opinion of someone who wears such awful clothes?

(2) **Straw man** is a kind of argument that pretends to refute or defeat an opposing view by misrepresenting it as a different view––usually one that is much more extreme and easier to refute than the actual argument. For example:

> A: I think we need more data before we can conclude that human activity is causing global warming.
> B: People who dispute global warming care nothing for future generations. Thus, if you do care about future generations, you should not listen to those who question global warming.

(3) **Slippery slope** is a kind of argument that states that a relatively small first step will necessarily lead to a much more serious situation; yet it gives no explanation for how this will actually happen. For example:

> If we allow the university to raise tuition by five percent this year, there's nothing to stop them from raising it again every year. Pretty soon, students will be paying twice as much!

---

❶ Match the arguments (on the left) with the type of fallacy that they represent (on the right).

1 Should we allow governments to have access to our private information? Well, if you are not doing anything wrong, then what do you have to worry about?
•   • **a.** *Ad hominem*

2 Senator Robertson wants to give police the right to search your email without just cause. Just last year, he was caught for misusing his expense account on personal matters. Why should we believe him?
•   • **b.** Slippery slope

3 Denying the government the right to search email and track Internet use will only make life easy for terrorists and drug dealers.
•   • **c.** Straw man

❷ Read the two excerpts from Reading 2. Underline the fallacy and check the correct type of fallacy. Then write a short counter-argument.

1 The act still allows government officials to collect personal data, including background, education, and health records. Also, they are not required to inform the person who is being monitored. As such, critics say that nothing has changed and that supporters of the PDPA have no concern for protecting privacy.

☐ *Ad hominem*   ☐ Slippery slope   ☐ Straw man

Counter-argument: _____

_____

2 They even argue that citizens should not give up any amount of privacy. Otherwise, the government would take away more and more privacy rights until there is none left. Hypothetically, this would create a world in which governments spy on their citizens' every move.

☐ *Ad hominem*   ☐ Slippery slope   ☐ Straw man

Counter-argument: _____

_____

VOCABULARY REVIEW

Fill in the blanks with the correct words from the box. Change the form of the word if necessary.

clause	coherent	compound	constitution
hypothetically	inviolable	suspend	terminate

1 Human life is _____, so no one should take another person's life.

2 Each country has its own _____, which states all of the rights that its citizens have.

3 If you were the principal, _____ speaking, would you do away with school uniforms?

4 The judge decided to _____ the man's driver's license because he had too many speeding tickets.

5 Education budget cuts _____ the problem because the school district already did not have enough funds.

6 If you can't make a(n) _____ argument, you won't stand a chance in the debate.

7 The act has a(n) _____ that requires every person 18 years and older to vote in national elections.

8 He was _____ after being caught stealing money from the company.

WW Go to page 196 of the Skills Handbook for the Writing Worksheet.

12 Cities of the Future

How urban designers are changing the world we live in

Think About It

What are some changes you'd like to see made to your city?

A great city is that which has the greatest men and women.

Walt Whitman

What you'll learn in this unit:

Reading 1 / Five Routes to the Future
Reading Skill: Determining the Author's Purpose

Reading 2 / Urban Design: The Need for Green Spaces
Critical Thinking Skill: Evaluating Arguments

Unit Project | **Make Your Point**
Describe changes that you would like to see in your city

Before You Read

1 **What aspects of your city do you like? What do you dislike? Discuss with a partner. Use the list below or your own ideas.**

- People
- Architecture
- Natural environment
- Weather

- Public facilities
- Sports and recreation facilities
- Transport and parking facilities
- Other (specify)

2 **Imagine your ideal city. Where would it be located? What are two aspects of your ideal city that you could not live without? Share with a partner. You can use these photos for ideas.**

A

B

VOCABULARY PREVIEW

Match each AWL word in bold with its meaning from the box.

> a. the building process
> c. a way of doing something
> e. the act of using up
> g. creative and new
>
> b. a connected system
> d. a basic structure underlying a concept
> f. laws passed by a government
> h. capable of continuing for a long time

_____ **1** For a community to be **sustainable**, it must balance human needs with the environment.

_____ **2** Urban planners created a **framework** to guide the city's development project.

_____ **3** The city developed **innovative** policies to protect the environment.

_____ **4** **Construction** of the light railway system took into consideration the environment.

_____ **5** A **network** of underground pipes transports the city's waste to a treatment facility.

_____ **6** The city decided to use a different **mode** of collecting the local community's opinions.

_____ **7** People can use the technology to measure their daily energy **consumption**.

_____ **8** The city passed environmental **legislation** in support of green solutions.

READING PREVIEW

This passage is an article about environmentally friendly cities.

> Many modern cities have convenient facilities for residents that are designed to reduce society's negative effects on the environment. What are some examples that you know? Write a list and share it with a partner.

Track 23

Five Routes to the Future

by Kate Morris
© 2014, Guardian News and Media Limited. Used by permission.

Q What is the main point of the passage? Underline it.

At first glance[1], a multimillion dollar property development in South Korea does not have much in common with one of Europe's oldest settlements. But what unites Songdo and Nice, along with the three other cities featured here, is a willingness to take on new ideas and a bold approach to implementing them. Nice, Medellín Songdo, Portland, and Coventry have a particular vision of becoming world leaders in urban planning and [5] models for cutting carbon emissions[2]. And they are going about it in a "smart" way.

Songdo, South Korea

Central Park in Songdo is South Korea's model for green cities.

Imagine a city with no traffic jams, where air conditioning, heating, and lights can be controlled from a mobile phone or computer. Video-conferencing screens in every apartment [10] and "green meters" allow residents to track their daily energy **consumption**.

This is smart life in Songdo, South Korea, the private $35 million (£21.5 million) development founded in August 2009 on a man-made island in the Yellow Sea. It is expected to have a population of 65,000 and [15] up to 300,000 daily commuters[3].

Forty percent of Songdo is green space, including a 100-acre park at the heart of the city. Water taxis are already navigating the city's seawater canal[4] system, and a bicycle rental system is to start next year on the city's 25 kilometers of bicycle lanes.

All offices, retail shops, and homes are constructed to strict environmental standards. [20] While a **network** of pipes removes solid waste, used city water and rain are collected for irrigation[5] and are recycled.

Q What is Songdo's solution to traffic problems?

And how will they stop traffic jams? Controllers will track people as they make journeys across the city and, by studying previous trips, will trigger the traffic lights as needed.
[25]

Portland, US

Portland, home to around 500,000 people in the north-western US, is leading the way in smart and **innovative** environmental **legislation**. It also ranks in the top ten green cities in the world. "We find when you focus on helping people live an easier, more robust[6] life, the environment wins, too," says Susan Anderson, the director of the city's department of planning and sustainability.
[30]

Q What role did the Portland community play in the construction of the light railway system?

The resolve of its residents to lead a more environmentally smart lifestyle dates back to the 1970s. At that time, community-led protests forced a switch of public money from a new freeway to a light railway system. Opened in 1986, the 52-mile railway is now hailed[7] as a model of environmentally friendly **construction** practices.

---

[1] **glance** *n.* a quick look
[2] **carbon emissions** *n.* gases that are released when burning fossil fuels like oil or coal
[3] **commuter** *n.* a person who travels regularly between two points, usually home and workplace

[4] **canal** *n.* a man-made channel of water used by boats or to carry water to crops
[5] **irrigation** *n.* the act of supplying water to land or crops
[6] **robust** *adj.* strong, healthy, and full of energy
[7] **hail** *v.* to give enthusiastic approval or praise for someone or something

35 In 1993, Portland became the first US local authority[8] to adopt a plan to reduce climate change. By 2009, total carbon dioxide emissions in the region were two percent below 1990 national levels and fifteen percent below 2000 levels, despite rapid growth of the city.

Last year, the city signed on to the EV (electric vehicle) Project, the largest such plan in
40 the world, according to Ecotality, the company behind it. An initial thirty-six charging stations in the city will grow to five hundred by next year.

Coventry, UK

This summer, Coventry, in the West Midlands, hit on a new **mode** of using technology to gather the opinions of its residents. Partnering with IBM, it held a three-day mass online
45 conversation—called CovJam, between some 3,000 residents, politicians, and council officers. The ideas that emerged from this discussion are now being used to reshape the authority's **sustainable** communities strategy.

Becoming the first UK local authority to launch such an online session demonstrates the council's desire to "take risks and innovate." It also reflects the city's position as a high-
50 tech center with local science parks and two universities—Warwick and Coventry—that specialize in advanced research.

A long-time supporter of alternative sources of energy, the city council bought its first electric vehicle back in 1995. Coventry is also one of only six UK authorities signed on to the government's Low-Carbon Vehicle Procurement Programme. Now the city has forty-
55 five low-carbon vehicles for various public service tasks.

Another local business, Microcab, is making cars powered by hydrogen. The city also boasts[9] eighteen electric charging stations and a hydrogen refueling station, one of only a handful in the country.

Medellín, Colombia

60 Medellíns £44.5 million cable car system carrying those living in the sprawling barrios above the city to its center is more than just an integrated transport project.

The cable cars are at the centre of a unique social and urban development **framework** that has helped reduce the Colombian city's high murder rate. This demonstrates how "smart" projects can help solve social issues.

65 It was led by the city's then mayor Sergio Fajardo and a team of experts in various fields, who believed integrating the city's poor was central to reducing gang violence.

The first cable cars started running in 2004, offering residents in the barrio of Santo Domingo a seven-minute ride to the centre of Medellín. This dramatically shortened their journey, which previously took one or two hours by minibus.

70 Over the following four years, a second line was constructed. In addition, libraries and child-care facilities have been built in and around the cable car stations in the distant towns.

While crime remains a problem in Medellín, the murder rate has more than halved from 3,557 in 2002 to 1,717 last year.

Nice, France

75 Nice has become the first European city to use near-field communication (NFC) technology to permit payment at public places. People in Nice can now make purchases at shops, museums, and galleries, as well as on trams and buses, via smart phones. The ultimate goal is to end the use of paper or plastic money to pay for various local goods and services.

Q What environmental technology do the cities of Portland and Coventry have in common?

C Medellín's new urban design is said to result in decreased crime. What evidence is used to prove this?

---

8 **authority** *n.* a person or institution that has the power or control in a situation

9 **boast** *v.* to have, or feature, something positive

At the moment, only Samsung phones, available from four local networks, have the NFC chip. But the hope is that eventually it will be on all new mobiles. Also, fifteen more French cities are considering following Nice's example. [80]

Christian Estrosi, the mayor of Nice and minister for industry in the French government, says he believes strongly in making the city an area where innovation can grow. "Innovation improves the well-being of our people, as well as triggering growth and jobs for the future." [85]

Reading 1

 ○ Comprehension

MAPPING IDEAS

Organize the ideas from Reading 1. Review the passage and fill in the graphic organizer below.

Green cities of the future

Songdo
- Use [1] _____ on the city's waterways
- Collect and [2] _____ rain and waste water

Portland
- In the top ten [3] _____ worldwide
- Promote use of [4] _____ for vehicles

[5] _____
- High-tech center with science parks and universities
- Has one of a few [6] _____ in UK

Medellín
- Serve barrios with _____ system
- Built _____ and child-care facilities

Nice
- Enable _____ technology for purchases
- Replace _____ money for payments

R W | Before you go on, boost your reading skills. Go to page 198 of the Skills Handbook.

○ Comprehension

FOCUS ON CONTENT

❶ **Circle the main idea of the passage. For each of the other sentences, check the reason it is not the main idea.**

1 Transportation is a major consideration in green city design.
☐ too general   ☐ too specific   ☐ not in passage   ☐ inaccurate

2 Five cities are taking different approaches to increase the use of green technology.
☐ too general   ☐ too specific   ☐ not in passage   ☐ inaccurate

3 New urban designs show the connection between green spaces and human health.
☐ too general   ☐ too specific   ☐ not in passage   ☐ inaccurate

4 In the future, city planners have to consider environmental impact.
☐ too general   ☐ too specific   ☐ not in passage   ☐ inaccurate

② Check the statements that are true according to the passage. Correct the false statements.

1 ☐ Currently, not all cell phones in Nice have near-field communication chips.

_____

2 ☐ Portland and Coventry both have a light railway system.

_____

3 ☐ Funding for the development of Songdo is primarily from government investment.

_____

4 ☐ Medellín is an example of how urban design can also be used to solve social problems.

_____

③ Choose the best answer.

1 What did the cable car system do for Santo Domingo in Colombia?
   a. It reduced carbon emissions because fewer people now drive cars.
   b. It cut down the commuting time to Medellín to seven minutes.
   c. It was the main reason for Mayor Sergio Fajardo's re-election.
   d. It increased the city's revenue by tens of millions of pounds.

2 Where did the ideas come from for reshaping Coventry's sustainable communities strategy?
   a. A committee of experts in consultation with the mayor
   b. A study of models that worked in other cities
   c. A survey of customers at local restaurants and shops
   d. An online discussion that involved various community members

THINK AND DISCUSS

① Read the excerpt from the reading passage.

> But what unites Songdo and Nice, along with the three other cities featured here, is a willingness to take on new ideas and a bold approach to implementing them. Nice, Medellín, Songdo, Portland, and Coventry have a particular vision of becoming world leaders in urban planning and models for cutting carbon emissions.

Discuss the following questions with a partner.

• Which of the innovations described in the passage have you heard of before? Which have you not heard of before?
• Which of the cities would you like to live in? Why?

❷ Read the following situation and write a short response.

> • Building a new light railway system
> • Replacing all government vehicles with electric ones
> • Starting a bike rental system in public parks

However, there is only enough money in the budget to do one of the options. Which one would you choose and why?

_____

_____

_____

_____

VOCABULARY REVIEW

Fill in the blanks with the correct words from the box. Change the form of the word if necessary.

construction	consumption	framework	innovative
legislation	mode	network	sustainable

1 Successful corporations must have an organized _____ for structuring their human resources.

2 Your business won't be _____ if your costs stay high and you don't have good staff.

3 I was told that _____ of the building would be delayed because of budget cutbacks.

4 Congress passed new _____ that increased the minimum wage nationwide.

5 The subway line is closed for repairs today, so use a different _____ of transportation.

6 Scuba divers must pay attention to their oxygen _____ while they are underwater.

7 My role in the company is to suggest _____ business ideas for clients to invest in.

8 Melted snow from the Rocky Mountains is the main water source for the _____ of rivers and lakes in the region.

Reading 2

VOCABULARY PREVIEW

Read the sentence. Circle the choice that is closest to the meaning of the AWL word in bold.

1 The city's **infrastructure** is a mix of concrete structures and green spaces.
   a. road system
   b. basic structures
   c. underground pipes

2 The study looked at various forms of **misconduct** that residents committed.
   a. offense
   b. behavior
   c. investigation

3 Residents have a greater **appreciation** for the area they live in if it has green spaces.
   a. gratitude
   b. neglect
   c. awareness

4 The **revolution** of ideas for new types of green spaces is spreading across the country.
   a. rotation
   b. major remodeling
   c. major change

5 People need a way to **offset** the hard urban landscape with greenery.
   a. approve
   b. balance
   c. redirect

6 The goal of the project **coincides** with the findings of studies.
   a. motivates
   b. corresponds
   c. differs

7 Studies show that greenery can lead to a decrease in the **occurrence** of crime in the area.
   a. happening
   b. refusal
   c. protection

8 Covering **external** walls with vegetation protects the building.
   a. remote
   b. inner
   c. outer

READING PREVIEW

This passage is about the use of green spaces in urban design.

What are some of the benefits of having green spaces in cities? Make a list of them and share it with a partner.

Read the passage.

Urban Design: The Need for Green Spaces

by Jon Maes / Language Cradle Consulting

Q What are some effects of green spaces on learning and working environments? Underline them.

The University of Guelph-Humber in Toronto, Canada, is gaining recognition in the world of academia[1] because of its indoor "living wall." Students, employees, and visitors to the campus praise the four-story plant construction for its visual appeal and ingenuity[2]. In fact, the university's decision to build the living wall **coincides** with studies that show the positive impacts green spaces have on learning and working environments. For example, scientific data indicates that plants enhance student and employee satisfaction, which results in decreased absenteeism[3] and increased productivity.

Q What does the author say city planners need to do?

Greenery has positive effects on learning and working environments.

The positive impact of greenery on school environments is only one aspect of the green **revolution** that has been taking place over the past few decades. Increasingly, green spaces are changing the character of cities and enriching[4] people's lives in various ways. However, not everyone agrees. The challenge now is to persuade all city planners to **offset** the concrete coldness of many downtown neighborhoods with areas of greenery, such as parks, gardens, and arboretums[5].

Unfortunately, the sections of cities that have the greatest need for greenery are also the places where it is most difficult to find room for it. City planners then must be creative and inventive when incorporating greenery into existing **infrastructures**.

Green roofs are an innovation that is becoming more commonplace in major cities. A famous green roof in the US is found on top of the Chicago City Hall. It covers an area of 20,300 square feet with native plants from the Midwest region. There is also the International Hall in Fukuoka, Japan. This government building is made up of fifteen terraces[6] with 35,000 plants representing seventy-six different species.

Q What innovation does Parkhill in Bratislava share with Chicago and Fukuoka?

Another example is an award-winning design in Bratislava, Slovakia, called the Parkhill. Architects were given the task of meeting the city's need for more housing and public spaces without taking away the urban forest surrounding the city center. Their solution made use of green roofs similar to those in Chicago and Fukuoka and included courtyards and vertical gardens along with 350 apartments, dozens of offices, and a hotel—all built on the hillside.

Green spaces do more than just create better learning and working environments.

---

[1] **academia** *n.* the community concerned with the pursuit of knowledge and study

[2] **ingenuity** *n.* the quality or instance of being very smart; cleverness

[3] **absenteeism** *n.* repeated absence from a place where regular attendance is required, such as work or school

[4] **enrich** *v.* to make more interesting, important, or rewarding

[5] **arboretum** *n.* a place where trees are grown for study or display

[6] **terrace** *n.* a flat, raised section of ground

They offer many other advantages for cities and the environment. Certain plants act as natural filters by removing chemicals and toxins from the air. Plants also help decrease indoor temperatures by blocking out the sun. They can even protect **external** walls from weather damage. Building owners should be happy to hear this. Think of the savings they can make. Moreover, plants provide a habitat for birds, squirrels, and other urban wildlife.

Additionally, in cities that receive heavy rainfall, vegetation absorbs some of the water and prevents sewer systems from becoming overloaded. And because leaves have the ability to trap sound, plants can act as a noise reducer, so having green spaces in densely populated areas helps muffle[7] street noise.

Experts have also found a connection between the amount of greenery in the environment and crime rates. Green spaces, it seems, decrease stress, anxiety, and aggression in people, which in turn leads to a reduction in the **occurrence** of violence. Indeed, a study of apartments by the city of Chicago found that greenery can lessen crime by as much as fifty percent, including littering[8], vandalism[9], and other acts of criminal **misconduct**. Part of the reason for this reduction is that residents have more **appreciation** for the area they live in. Green areas also attract people to go there, and the large number of potential eyewitnesses can be a deterrent to criminals.

In addition to reducing crime, green spaces can actually support the local economy. Research from the University of Washington indicates that shopping districts with trees and gardens are more appealing to customers. In particular, surveys determined that customers spent 9 to 12 percent more time in shopping districts with greenery than in those without. Psychologically, landscaping[10] also has the effect of making people think that the quality of goods and services is higher because of the impression that extra attention is being given to the shopping environment. This results in more shopping and more buying, which is sure to make any store owner happy.

All in all, the importance of having green spaces in public areas is becoming increasingly clear. As human populations grow, cities expand, which exerts pressure on the natural surroundings. City planners should find innovative ways of building green spaces into urban designs because the benefits to our society and the environment are too great to ignore. With such impressive green spaces serving as models, it will be interesting to see how people will use nature to transform cities in the future.

C What does the author infer about building owners with regard to green spaces?

Q How can green spaces help the local economy?

---

[7] **muffle** *v.* to make quieter by using a covering of some sort

[8] **littering** *n.* a type of crime involving trash being scattered in public places instead of being properly disposed of

[9] **vandalism** *n.* a type of crime involving purposeful damage to property

[10] **landscape** *v.* to change a piece of land by adding plants and other features to make it more attractive

Reading 2

FOCUS ON CONTENT

1 **Choose the best answer.**

1 What is the passage mainly about?
- a. City planning as it relates to environmental protection
- b. The reasons that modern cities must have green spaces
- c. Considerations for planting vegetation indoors and outdoors
- d. The use of natural environments in award-winning urban designs

2 All of the following are advantages of green spaces mentioned in the passage EXCEPT:
- a. helping the local economy by creating jobs
- b. providing homes for native animals
- c. reducing flooding in places with heavy rainfall
- d. deterring residents from committing crimes

3 According to the passage, what is one way that having green spaces can reduce crime?
- a. It gives people more places to hide from violent criminals in their neighborhood.
- b. It helps the local economy, so people have more money.
- c. It attracts more people to the area, so criminals are more worried about getting caught.
- d. It creates more activities for people to participate in so they do not cause trouble.

4 Which of the following statements about shoppers would the author most likely agree with?
- a. They are more concerned about prices than the landscaping.
- b. They notice when store owners decorate their stores with greenery.
- c. They are more likely to visit shopping areas that have green spaces.
- d. They tend to shop near their homes regardless of the urban design.

5 How can plants help protect buildings?
- a. By absorbing the water that does not soak into the ground
- b. By protecting the walls from overexposure to sunlight
- c. By decreasing the amount of litter in the area
- d. By keeping animals away

2 **Complete the sentences with information from the passage.**

1 Shopping districts with greenery give people the impression that _____.

2 The green roof on top of the Chicago City Hall only uses plants from _____.

3 It is difficult to build green spaces in some city sections because _____.

4 Evidence that living walls improve learning and working environments includes
_____.

5 Green spaces are said to make people feel less _____.

IDEAS IN ACTION

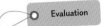

Talk about the questions with a partner.

1   Do you agree with the author's argument that green spaces can help reduce crime? Why or why not?

2   What are some possible disadvantages of building green spaces in cities? Explain.

CRITICAL THINKING

Evaluating Arguments

Whenever an author's purpose is to persuade, it's important to critically evaluate the argument that he or she puts forward. These are what you need to examine:

(1) Author's position: First, identify the position that the author is trying to convince readers of. The author may be trying to persuade readers to adopt or reject an idea, or to take or refrain from a certain action.

(2) Method of persuasion: Next, focus on *how* the author is trying to persuade readers. He or she may be using an argument of some kind, but there may also be emotionally charged or biased language, which should be ignored. If an argument is presented, it may be worthwhile to highlight it or write it out to make it easier to evaluate.

(3) Validity of the argument: Then, look carefully at the argument itself. Try to identify whether it is inductive or deductive. If it is deductive, make sure that the form is valid. Are there any subarguments? Are there any important assumptions made?

(4) Truth of the premises and their support: Are the premises true? Can you recognize any fallacies? Try to identify what kind of claims the author is making. Which are provable facts and which are merely opinions? You also need to closely examine the evidence that the author gives to support the premises. It's important that it comes from reliable sources. Statistics and research studies should be examined with a critical eye.

If the argument is valid and the premises are true and well-supported, then the argument is reasonable and you're justified in being convinced by it.

Read the excerpt from Reading 2. Then answer the questions.

In addition to reducing crime, green spaces can actually support the local economy. Research from the University of Washington indicates that shopping districts with trees and gardens are more appealing to customers. In particular, surveys determined that customers spent 9 to 12 percent more time in shopping districts with greenery than in those without. Psychologically, landscaping also has the effect of making people think that the quality of goods and services is higher because of the impression that extra attention is being given to the shopping environment. This results in more shopping and more buying, which is sure to make any store owner happy.

1   What is the author's position in this paragraph? Rewrite the argument in your own words.

2 How does the author try to persuade readers about the argument? Identify statements in the paragraph that use persuasion, and check the type of persuasion method used. Then summarize the statement(s) for each type.

a. ☐ Appeal to the reader's emotions

_____

b. ☐ Expert opinion or authority on the subject

_____

c. ☐ Evidence, data, or statistics

_____

d. ☐ Logical reasoning

_____

3 What assumption does the author make about customers in shopping districts?

a. People prefer to shop in places with lots of greenery.

b. Most people do not go shopping with something to buy in mind.

c. People shop and buy more when they are in a good mood.

d. Landscaping attracts more affluent shoppers.

4 Which statement(s) does the author make that are provable facts? Which are merely opinions? Explain.

_____

5 After analyzing the excerpt, do you find the author's argument persuasive? Why or why not?

_____

VOCABULARY REVIEW

Match each word to its definition.

1 appreciation (n.) •   • **a** the basic structure of a place, organization, system, etc.

2 coincide (v.) •   • **b** to make up for; to balance

3 external (adj.) •   • **c** to be the same in some respect; to agree

4 infrastructure (n.) •   • **d** a very great change

5 misconduct (n.) •   • **e** an event that takes places; an incident

6 occurrence (n.) •   • **f** of the outside or outer part

7 offset (v.) •   • **g** wrong or bad behavior that is often unlawful or against rules

8 revolution (n.) •   • **h** a feeling or expression of thanks

WW Go to page 199 of the Skills Handbook for the Writing Worksheet.

SKILLS WORKBOOK

Compass
Publishing

CONTENTS

Reading Skills Worksheet

Unit
1

Analysis

Previewing and Predicting

Previewing and predicting is a strategy in which readers actively think about what they are going to read based on clues from the text combined with their own background knowledge. Then, as they read, they either confirm or revise their predictions. In this way, readers' minds are focused on the topic and are better prepared to take in information.

Before you read a passage, look at the title, photos and captions, and section headings (if any). Look at the first sentence of each paragraph. Ask yourself what clues they give you to the content of the passage.

As you read, think about whether your initial predictions were correct, and ask yourself what is likely to come next in the passage.

1 **Look at the title, photos, and photo captions of Reading 1. Then fill in the chart.**

Clue	Prediction
"Early Adopters Fall into a Costly Trap"	☐ 1. The author's view of early adopters is probably _____.
"To be an early adopter is to throw your money away."	☐ 2. The author might talk about _____ _____.
	☐ 3. _____ _____

2 **Read the beginning of paragraph 3. Then answer the question.**

Speaking of becoming obsolete, those who are first to leap into a new technology risk wasting money and time on something that will never catch on.

What do you think the author will discuss in the rest of the paragraph? Make a prediction.

☐ Prediction: The author will discuss _____

_____.

3 **After you read Reading 1, check (✔) which predictions that you made above were correct.**

📖 Writing Worksheet

Synthesis

Use the worksheet below to develop your response to the following question.

Do you think it is a good idea to be an early adopter of technology?

| **Opinion 1** | Yes, I think it is a good idea to be an early adopter of technology. |

Reason 1   Your career benefits when you stay up-to-date with the latest technological devices and trends.

Explanation/Example _____

_____

Reason 2 _____

Refer to Reading 2, paragraph 2, on page 10 for some ideas.

Explanation/Example _____

_____

Reason 3 _____

Refer to Reading 2, paragraph 4, on page 11 for some ideas.

Explanation/Example _____

_____

Counter-argument   It is true that buying devices when they first come out means that you pay more for them.

Refutation _____

_____

| **Conclusion**   Overall, the gains from being an early adopter far outweigh the costs. |

☐ **Opinion 2** No, I do not think it is a good idea to be an early adopter of technology.

Reason 1 Brand-new technology hasn't been thoroughly tested and often has problems.

Explanation/Example _____

_____

Use your answers to Think and Discuss on page 7.

Reason 2 _____

Explanation/Example _____

_____

Reason 3 _____

Use your answers to Reading Preview on page 3.

Explanation/Example _____

_____

Counter-argument The discounts and other rewards offered by tech companies to early adopters are certainly attractive.

Refutation _____

_____

Conclusion As such, consumers can save time and money by waiting until the new technology is fully proven and its price drops.

 **Reading Skills Worksheet**

 Analysis

Analyzing the Author's Point of View

Active reading requires the reader to recognize the author's point of view. This allows critical consideration of the perspective(s) presented, which helps the reader determine if those perspectives are valid, fully supported, objective, and persuasive.

When looking for and analyzing the author's point of view, consider the following:
- What is the author's main point for the paragraph or passage?
- What, if anything, does the author have to gain from convincing readers of the main point?
- What evidence does the author give to support that point of view? Is that evidence valid?
- What valid counter-evidence does the author fail to present or address? Why?

1 **Refer back to Reading 1. Circle the correct answers and then answer the follow-up questions to critically analyze the author's point of view.**

(1) Which of the following statements would the author most likely agree with?
  a. All students should take both academic and vocational subjects.
  b. Flexible education methods are better suited for private schools than for public schools.
  c. Ideal school environments have small class sizes to foster more teacher-student interaction.
  d. The funding that a school receives should be based on its students' level of academic achievement.

What information does the author give to support this statement? Do you think the author's support is adequate? Explain why or why not.

_____

_____

(2) All of the following sentences support the author's opinion about the Finnish education system EXCEPT:
  a. Free education is essential to ensure all children have access to an education.
  b. Most teachers need to receive further training from the government.
  c. Students will develop the necessary skills if they are allowed to be independent learners.
  d. Having lessons that mix more than one academic discipline is effective.

How do you know that the author disagrees with this statement? Do you think the author gives enough support to disprove it? Explain why or why not.

_____

_____

2 **Read the following summary. Then write the author's point of view in one sentence.**

One of the biggest contrasts between education in Finland and the UK is in regard to public and private schools. There are very few private schools in Finland because every type of school is funded by the government and private schools are not permitted to charge fees. On the other hand, a significant portion of children in England go to private schools, with their parents thousands and thousands of pounds a year for them to attend. This creates unequal access to education in England that simply is not found in Finland, where all children have the same educational opportunities.

Author's point of view: _____

Writing Worksheet

Use the worksheet below to develop your response to the following question.

Based on the readings, what do you think are ideal conditions for students to learn in?

Opinion 1 I believe that Singapore's approach provides ideal conditions for student learning. The main elements of this approach include teaching by qualified instructors, _____, and _____.

Main idea 1 Qualified teachers are essential to any productive classroom.

Explanation/Example _____

_____

Main idea 2 _____

Refer to Reading 2 on pages 24 and 25 for some ideas.

Explanation/Example _____

_____

Main idea 3 _____

Explanation/Example _____

_____

Counter-argument Despite its success, Singapore's education system has been criticized for being too strict and too hard on students.

Refutation _____

_____

Conclusion For these reasons, I believe that Singapore's education system stands as a model for other countries to follow.

Opinion 2 Finland has an impressive education system that produces some of the best students in the world. It creates ideal conditions for learning through substantial government funding, _____, and _____.

Main idea 1 No student is left behind in Finland because the government makes education and meals free for students from kindergarten through university.

Explanation/Example _____

_____

Main idea 2 _____

Explanation/Example _____

_____

> Refer to Reading 1 on pages 18 and 19 for some ideas.

Main idea 3 _____

Explanation/Example _____

_____

Counter-argument Some critics argue that this approach is too loose because students and schools need structure to guide them properly.

Refutation _____

_____

Conclusion Finland's rise to the top of the education ladder shows that its education model of full government support coupled with teaching and learning flexibility works extremely well.

Reading Skills Worksheet

 Analysis

Asking Questions While Reading

Thoroughly comprehending a passage requires readers to be curious and thoughtful. Successful readers actively ask questions about the text and think about the answers as they continue reading. This helps clarify the author's intent, the ideas presented in the passage, as well as any connections between, or implications of, those ideas.

As you read, make a mental note of questions that occur to you and try to come up with answers. Such questions might include:

- What does this unfamiliar word mean?
- Why did the author choose this word or expression?
- How does the author support this point?
- Is this a good example of the author's point?
- Do I agree with this assertion?
- If this argument is correct, what might that mean?

1 **Read the excerpt from Reading 1. The numbers mark places where questions might occur to a thoughtful reader. Discuss the questions with a partner.**

The conventional workday is ideal for one type of person in particular: the early bird. (1) Research shows that genetic factors determine the length of a person's circadian (2) cycle, the series of biochemical signals that influence the body's rise and fall in energy levels and trigger drowsiness, wakefulness, hunger, etc. This cycle determines whether someone is an early bird or a night owl, according to Katherine Sharkey, a professor at Brown University and the associate director of the Sleep for Science Research Lab. (3) If your cycle is a bit shorter, you're most likely an early bird and the 9-to-5 routine suits you just fine. When you come in to work in the morning, you're all fired up and ready to go; and by the end of the day, your energy level starts to drop off.

But what if, like a sizable proportion of the population, you are more productive later in the day or even at night? The 9-to-5 routine forces night owls to try to be productive at times when their alertness and energy level are lowest.

(1) How does the author support this point?
(2) What does *circadian* mean?
(3) Is this appeal to authority persuasive?

2 **Write at least one more question you might ask while reading this excerpt. Discuss your question(s) with a partner.**

Q: _____

_____

Writing Worksheet

Use the worksheet below to develop your response to the following question.

> What should today's employers do to make sure their employees are productive and happy?

☐ **Opinion**   To make employees happy and productive, I think employers should allow flexible schedules, _____, and _____.

Main idea 1   Employers should allow flexible schedules.

Explanation/Example   _____

_____

Main idea 2   _____

Use your answers to Think and Discuss on page 35.

Explanation/Example   _____

_____

Main idea 3   _____

Use your answers to Ideas in Action on page 41.

Explanation/Example   _____

_____

Counter-argument   You might think that money is the most important thing a company can offer.

Refutation   _____

_____

Conclusion   Following the above recommendations will help companies promote productivity and loyalty among employees.

Reading Skills Worksheet

 Analysis

Comparing and Contrasting

Comparing and contrasting are ways of describing how people, ideas, or things are alike or different. A **comparison** shows how things are similar. A **contrast** shows how things are different.

Sometimes, writers compare and contrast things or ideas to help define them. For example, a writer might compare and contrast spiders and beetles so that readers can have a better understanding of both. Other times, writers compare and contrast things or ideas in order to evaluate them. For example, a writer might compare and contrast two cancer treatments so that readers can decide which treatment is better.

Writers use **transition words** and phrases to note comparisons and contrasts in their writing.
- For comparing, writers use expressions such as *both, share, like, as, too, moreover,* and *in a similar way/fashion.*
- For contrasting, writers use expressions such as *in contrast, on the one hand . . . on the other hand, unlike, however,* and *while.*

---

❶ **Read the summary of Reading 1. Fill in the blanks with the correct transitions.**

Conventional Chemotherapy vs. Nanomedicine Conventional chemotherapy and nanomedicine <u>share</u> some similarities. For example, 1. _____ chemotherapy and nanomedicine can be used to treat cancer. In addition, they both use powerful drugs to destroy cancerous cells. However, the effects of the two treatments on the human body are very different. 2. _____, chemotherapy cannot target cancer cells. Therefore, it damages normal, healthy tissues. This leads to a number of serious side effects, including hair loss, nausea, and even problems with bone marrow. 3. _____, nanomedicine can target specific cancer cells. Tiny nanotubes filled with medicine travel through the bloodstream looking for these cells. Then, the medicine is released at the site of the cancer. In this way, side effects can be greatly reduced. Finally, 4. _____ chemotherapy is currently in use to treat cancer, nanomedicine has not yet been approved for use in humans.	~~share~~ on the one hand on the other hand both while

---

❷ **Now fill in the organizer with the numbers of the correct information.**

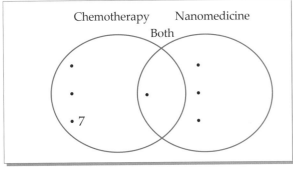

1. used to treat cancer
2. medicine placed inside microscopic tubes
3. delivers medicine directly to site of cancer
4. causes hair loss, nausea, and bone marrow problems
5. uses microwaves to release medicine
6. damages healthy body tissue
7. ~~associated with bad side effects~~

📖 Writing Worksheet

Synthesis

Use the worksheet below to develop your response to the following question.

In your opinion, what new invention or technology will have the greatest impact on human beings?

| **Opinion** | I think that advances in medical technology will transform human life more than any other technology will. |

Counter-argument   That's not to say that other technologies won't bring major

changes. _____

_____

Refutation _____

_____

Refer to Reading 1, paragraph 6, on page 47 for some ideas.

Reason 1   For one thing, the medical application of nanotechnology will extend people's lives.

Support _____

_____

_____

Refer to Reading 1, paragraph 7, on page 47 for some ideas.

Reason 2   Besides extending human life, nanotechnology can improve it as well.

Support _____

_____

_____

Conclusion _____

_____

Reading Skills Worksheet

Recalling and Extracting Information

It's always a good idea to see how much of a reading passage you actually understood. An easy way to do this is to try to **recall** the important points by quizzing yourself. Don't look back at the reading, and ask yourself some key questions like these:

- What is the topic of the reading?
- What is the author's main point?
- What are the most important reasons, facts, or details the author gives?

Answering these sorts of questions helps you to check whether you really understood the content. In addition, mentally reviewing the passage in this way helps you to remember it better.

If you find it hard to recall the information, you can **extract** it from the reading by skimming or scanning. You *skim a* reading to get general information about it (like the topic or main ideas) by looking through it quickly to get an overall idea of the content. On the other hand, you *scan* a reading to locate specific information (like dates, names, etc.).

1 **Close your student book and complete the following sentences.**

1. Reading 1 gives advice on how you can _____.

2. One piece of advice from the reading is that you should _____

_____.

3. The victim of the scam described in the last paragraph is a(n) _____.

2 **Open your student book to Reading 1. Skim or scan the reading to check your answers to exercise 1 above.**

3 **Scan Reading 1 to extract the answers to the following questions.**

1. How many people were fooled into paying for a fake apartment in Canada? Which paragraph did you find this information in?

_____; _____

2. What word does the author use to describe con artists' relationship history? Which paragraph did you find this information in?

_____; _____

Writing Worksheet

Use the worksheet below to develop your response to the following question.

What can people do to avoid being victims of con artists?

☐ **Opinion** To avoid being victims of con artists, people should guard their weaknesses, _____, and _____.

Main idea 1 People must constantly beware of con artists' tendency to prey on their targets' weaknesses.

Explanation/Example _____

_____

Refer to Reading 1, paragraph 5, on page 61 for some ideas.

Main idea 2 _____

Explanation/Example _____

_____

Use your answers to Ideas in Action on page 69.

Main idea 3 _____

Explanation/Example _____

_____

Counter-argument Some people say that certain con artists are so skilled that there is no way to avoid being tricked by them.

Refutation _____

_____

Conclusion Con artists are clever, but people can avoid becoming victims by being cautious, being aware of conmen's tricks, and being thorough in their research.

Reading Skills Worksheet

Making Inferences

Simply defined, **inference** is the act of guessing based on evidence and one's own knowledge. It is an essential reading skill because authors do not always give readers all the information. In such a case, readers need to infer by using the details included in the text together with their own experience to make a logical conclusion.

Here are some tips for making inferences:

- Find clues in the text by searching for essential information.
- Think about what information you already know about the topic.
- Note evidence and use logic to support your inference.
- Keep in mind that there is not always just one correct answer.

Read the following summaries of Reading 1. Then complete the charts.

(1) Mnemonics are much written about memory improvement techniques. You can find many titles on this topic in bookstores. They are the preferred method of some well-known memory masters. One mnemonic, called the loci method, involves associating things with familiar images that you visualize to help you recall these things more easily. The techniques have proven to be very effective.

Question	Given Information	Background Knowledge	Conclusion
What can be inferred about the popularity of mnemonics?	_____ _____ _____ _____	*I remember reading about mnemonics being used to help elderly people improve their memory, which has shown to be successful.*	_____ _____ _____ _____

(2) Evidence shows that students can improve their memory by adopting active learning methods such as repeated self-testing during their learning sessions outside class. This method has been found to be significantly more effective than just studying. Despite this, it is not something that students normally do, probably because it requires a great deal of effort.

Question	Given Information	Background Knowledge	Conclusion
Why do you think most students do not do self-testing?	_____ _____ _____ _____	_____ _____ _____ _____	_____ _____ _____ _____

Writing Worksheet

Synthesis

Use the worksheet below to develop your response to the following question.

Do you think you have a good memory? How do you think you could improve it?

Opinion In general, I would say that I have a good memory. but, there is always room for improvement. To enhance my memory, I could adopt more effective study habits, _____, and _____.

Main idea 1 Effective study methods improve information retention.

Explanation/Example _____

_____

Main idea 2 _____

> Refer to Reading 2 on pages 80 and 81 for some ideas.

Explanation/Example _____

_____

Main idea 3 _____

> Refer to Reading 1 on pages 74 and 75 for some ideas.

Explanation/Example _____

_____

Counter-argument My friends contend that my grades are already good and what I need to do to improve my memory is to rest more to reduce my stress levels.

Refutation _____

_____

Conclusion By using effective approaches to enhance my memory, I can spend less time on my study and have more time for other, more enjoyable activities.

Reading Skills Worksheet

Analysis

Identifying Causes and Effects

It is important to recognize how different ideas in a passage relate to one another, and one of the most common relationships between ideas is cause and effect. There are several different combinations of cause and effect. Here are the main ones:

(1) One cause, many effects (effect-focused)
The passage may explain the different effects that resulted from some action, event, or situation.

(2) One effect, many causes (cause-focused)
The passage may explain the different causes that led to some action, event, or situation.

(3) Chain of causation
The passage might show how several different events, actions, or situations lead from one to another.

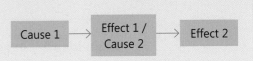

Read the statements based on Reading 1. In the empty space, draw a diagram to show the cause-and-effect relationship.

1 (A) Hambrick's study found that there was a big difference in the amount of practice among chess grandmasters and top musicians.

(B) Hambrick claimed the 10,000-hour rule is invalid.

(C) Hambrick's study found that deliberate practice only accounted for about thirty percent of success.

2 (A) Hambrick said that relying only on elite performers doesn't yield enough statistics.

(B) Hambrick studied a wide range of musicians and chess players.

(C) Ericsson said mixing data on people with different skill levels made Hambrick's criticism inappropriate.

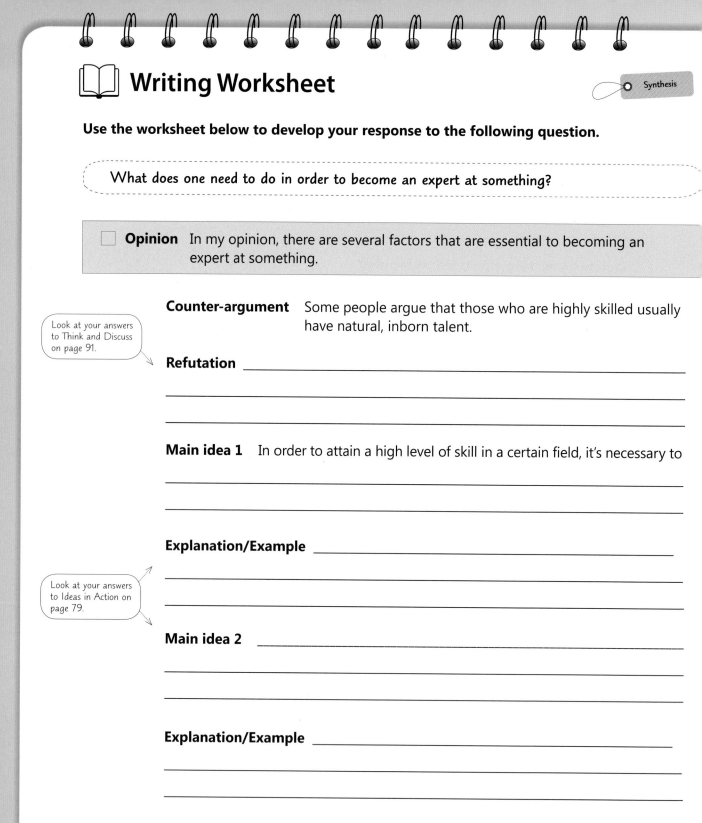

📖 Writing Worksheet

Synthesis

Use the worksheet below to develop your response to the following question.

What does one need to do in order to become an expert at something?

☐ **Opinion** In my opinion, there are several factors that are essential to becoming an expert at something.

Look at your answers to Think and Discuss on page 91.

Counter-argument Some people argue that those who are highly skilled usually have natural, inborn talent.

Refutation _____

_____

_____

Main idea 1 In order to attain a high level of skill in a certain field, it's necessary to

_____

_____

Explanation/Example _____

Look at your answers to Ideas in Action on page 79.

_____

_____

Main idea 2 _____

_____

_____

Explanation/Example _____

_____

_____

Conclusion While there may be other important factors, I believe these are the two most important that will help one become an expert.

Determining Importance

It is impossible—and unnecessary—to remember all the information in a passage. Authors include information that is intended to illustrate or clarify the important ideas, or even to just make the passage more entertaining. You do not have to remember all this information in detail. As you read, determine which parts of a text are most important and therefore most worth remembering.

The most important idea in a paragraph is often clearly stated in a topic sentence at the beginning or end of the paragraph. However, this is not always the case. Practice identifying the most important ideas in a paragraph by reading it a second time and highlighting, underlining, and/or taking notes on the parts that you want to remember.

In addition, authors sometimes signal importance through the use of italics, underlines, or bold. Pay extra attention to information that is presented in these ways.

Read the excerpts from Reading 1. In each, decide which information is the most important to the main idea of the passage and underline that information. Compare your choices with a partner's.

"That's partly because optimists are better at coping with setbacks and hardships," she adds. "When faced with a tough situation, optimists tend to respond with active problem-solving, positive thinking, and a sense of humor. Pessimists, on the other hand, tend to respond with hopelessness, denial, and avoidance. In the long run, this difference in coping style may mean that optimists experience less stress than pessimists do." Positive thinking is crucial to stress management, and going through life with the assumption that things will work out has numerous long-term health benefits.

. . .

Experts agree that too much pessimism can lead to hypochondria—the tendency to believe that a disease is present when it really is not. However, being a pessimist may provide an advantage when it comes to health prevention. "A pessimist is more likely to seek the advice of a professional. While in extreme cases this could lead to hypochondria, it could also lead to a potentially life-saving diagnosis," Cundy points out.

. . .

Both optimism and pessimism can impact health, but it seems both personalities could use a little bit of one another to really keep an individual at peak health. The optimist needs the caution of the pessimist, and the pessimist needs the drive of the optimist. "My father has always considered himself a 'guarded optimist,'" says Cundy. "He explains it this way: An optimist approaches a stop sign at a one way and only looks right. . . . A guarded optimist will approach the stop sign and look both ways not really expecting to see anyone—but, hey, how hard is it to look both ways?"

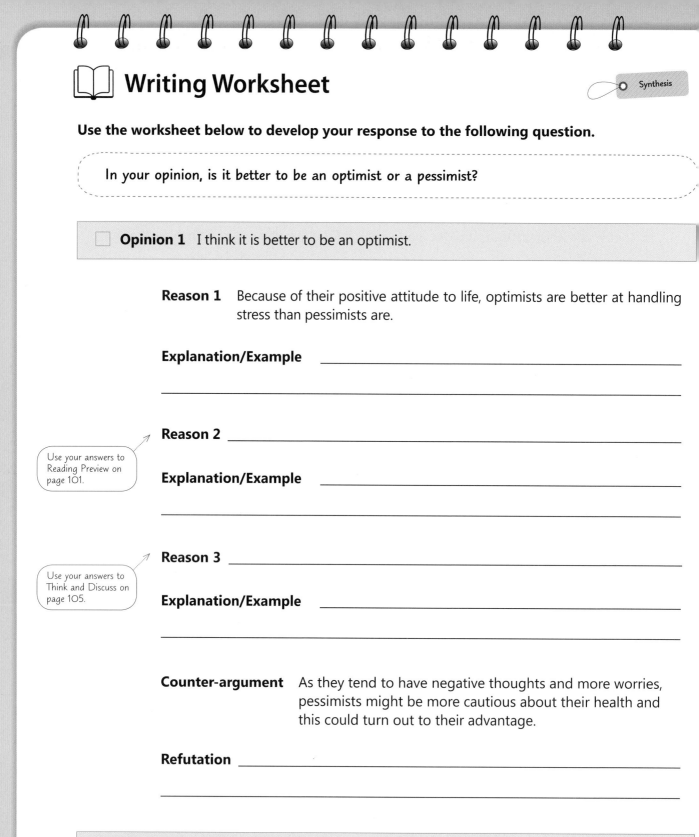

Writing Worksheet

Use the worksheet below to develop your response to the following question.

In your opinion, is it better to be an optimist or a pessimist?

Opinion 1 I think it is better to be an optimist.

Reason 1 Because of their positive attitude to life, optimists are better at handling stress than pessimists are.

Explanation/Example _____

_____

Reason 2 _____

Use your answers to Reading Preview on page 101.

Explanation/Example _____

_____

Reason 3 _____

Use your answers to Think and Discuss on page 105.

Explanation/Example _____

_____

Counter-argument As they tend to have negative thoughts and more worries, pessimists might be more cautious about their health and this could turn out to their advantage.

Refutation _____

_____

Conclusion Because it generally leads to good health and happiness, optimism is definitely preferable.

188

Opinion 2   I think it is a better idea to be a pessimist.

Reason 1   Pessimists probably live longer.

Explanation/Example _____

_____

Reason 2 _____

Explanation/Example _____

_____

Use your answers to Reading Preview on page 107.

Reason 3 _____

Explanation/Example _____

_____

Counter-argument   Evidence shows that optimists tend to have more friends because of their sunny personality.

Refutation _____

_____

Conclusion   In many ways, pessimism prepares a person for life's challenges better than optimism does.

 Analysis

Monitoring and Clarifying Understanding

One of the most important features that distinguish strong readers is the ability to recognize when they do not understand something. Strong readers know when they do not understand, can identify what they do not understand, and then reread part of a passage or seek clarification in other ways. Here are some strategies to use in seeking clarification:

- Stop periodically and think about what you are reading. Think about how you would explain to someone else what you have read.
- Reread parts of the text that you had trouble with at first.
- Guess the meaning of unfamiliar words, or look them up.
- Slow down or speed up your reading, depending on the difficulty of the text.
- Visualize what the text is discussing.
- Take a break and think about what you have read so far.
- Ask someone to explain anything that is still unclear.

1 **Read the following excerpt from Reading 1. As you read, underline any unfamiliar words or phrases and try to guess their meaning. If you can't guess it, use a dictionary.**

Today's parents tend to treat young adults like pampered teens, reinvesting in dormant parenting roles, especially if their kids are struggling. "The underlying message is 'We don't think you can do it on your own,'" says Marie Hartwell-Walker, psychologist and mother of four adult children, two of whom came home to live with her and her husband. This treatment prevents their kids from truly reaching maturity.

It's painful to recognize that adults cannot be reliant on their parents forever, and that many life lessons must be learned alone. This truth is compounded by baby boomers' refusal to acknowledge getting older, which sends an additional message to young adults that there will always be time to get another degree, to break up with one more partner or employer, to change direction. If parents aren't "old" (and with hair color and joint replacements, who doesn't want to pretend they're still 40?), then for adultescents, the years must be standing still. Parents of adult children need to step back so young adults can step forward.

2 **Discuss the following questions with a partner.**

1. Which words or phrases did you underline? Do you and your partner agree on their meaning?

2. Did you have to read any part of the excerpt more than once in order to understand it? Which part(s)?

3. In your own words, explain one of the following to your partner:

   a. How being pampered by their parents affects adult children

   b. The attitude of baby boomers toward aging

Writing Worksheet

Use the worksheet below to develop your response to the following question.

Do you think it's a good idea for young adults to live with their parents?

☐ **Opinion 1** In many cases, I think it's a good idea for young adults to live with their parents.

Reason 1 It can help them pay off their student loan debt much faster.

Explanation/Example _____

_____

Reason 2 _____

Use your answers to Think and Discuss on page 119.

Explanation/Example _____

_____

Reason 3 _____

Use your answers to Reading Preview on page 121.

Explanation/Example _____

_____

Counter-argument Experts say that living at home makes young adults less mature.

Refutation _____

_____

Conclusion In the right circumstances, living at home can benefit young adults enormously.

	Opinion 2 No, I do not think it's a good idea for young adults to live with their parents.

Reason 1   For one thing, it slows down the process of becoming a mature adult.

Explanation/Example _____

_____

> Use your answers to Reading Preview on page 115.

Reason 2 _____

Explanation/Example _____

_____

> Use your answers to Think and Discuss on page 119.

Reason 3 _____

Explanation/Example _____

_____

Counter-argument   Young adults often have to live on extremely tight budgets and have a hard time making ends meet.

Refutation _____

_____

Conclusion   For a young person, becoming independent is a difficult but necessary part of life, and it is well worth the effort.

Reading Skills Worksheet

Summarizing

Being able to summarize a passage is an important reading skill. When you **summarize** a text, briefly restate its main points—and only its main points—in your own words. This helps you focus on and remember the most important information from the passage.

When writing a summary, ask yourself these questions:

- What are the main ideas of the passage?
- Which information is crucial for supporting these main ideas?
- Which information is minor and can therefore be left out?

1 **Look at the information based on Reading 1. Cross out two details that are minor and can be left out of the summary.**

- US study asked pre-teens about serious offenses by friends and their reactions
- Girls reported more anger and sadness in their responses
- Authors were a professor and an assistant professor
- Past studies have said girls are better at friendship

- One story involved a bad grade on a school project
- Girls and boys were equally aggressive
- Girls may struggle more when friends disappoint them

2 **Use the remaining information to write a summary of the reading (3 to 5 sentences).**

Summary: Girls Feel More Anger When Friends Offend

_____

_____

_____

_____

_____

_____

_____

Writing Worksheet

Synthesis

Use the worksheet below to develop your response to the following question.

What are the main differences between male and female friendships?

Opinion Male and female friendships differ in three main ways: what friends do together, _____, and _____.

Main idea 1 Females tend to bond "face-to-face," while males tend to bond "shoulder-to-shoulder."

Explanation/Example _____

_____

Use your answers to Before You Read on page 128.

Main idea 2 _____

Explanation/Example _____

_____

Use your answers to Ideas in Action on page 139.

Main idea 3 _____

Explanation/Example _____

_____

Counter-argument It might appear that males do not value friendship as much as females do.

Refutation _____

_____

Conclusion Despite these differences, people of both sexes value and benefit from their friendships.

 Analysis

Facts and Opinions

Authors make statements that use facts and opinions when they write. **Facts** are statements that can be proven as true with supporting evidence. **Opinions** are statements that are a person's beliefs or feelings. Identifying facts and opinions helps readers to better understand what they are reading. Also, it is a skill for evaluating the points that the author is making. Readers use this skill to determine if the author's statements are persuasive or trustworthy. Here are some tips for distinguishing facts from opinions.

Fact:

- Is evidence provided to support the statement, or can the statement be verified? For example, are statistics, data, personal experiences, or common knowledge used as support?
- Is the person making the statement an expert on the topic being discussed?

Opinion:

- Are opinion words used, such as *think* or *believe*?
- Are there words used to describe feelings or beliefs like *pretty, ugly, easy, difficult, best,* or *worst*?

1 **Read the biography about the author of Reading 1 and answer the question.**

Siraj Datoo is a UK-based columnist who has been in journalism for over four years. He specializes in technology and business with his articles having been published in newspapers such as *The Guardian, The Telegraph, The Independent,* and the *Huffington Post*. He has also spoken on issues related to digital culture, politics, and technology for BBC World television and radio shows. While studying for a master's degree in Newspaper Journalism at City University London, he founded and served as editor of two online student periodicals.

From this biography, would you say that Siraj Datoo is a credible author for the topic of Reading 1? Why or why not?

_____

2 **Read the statements from Reading 1. Then circle *Fact* or *Opinion* and explain your choice.**

a. Euclid's is currently the only offline customer analytics platform that is available for free.

Fact / Opinion _____

_____

b. Emma Carr, a senior director at Big Brother Watch, believes that this technology ignores customers' privacy.

Fact / Opinion _____

_____

c. "I would think permission would need to be given to use something that belongs to someone else. Even if it is just a signal," one consumer posted on Facebook.

Fact / Opinion _____

_____

Writing Worksheet

Use the worksheet below to develop your response to the following question.

Is it OK for companies and other organizations to collect information about people?

☐ **Opinion 1** More often than not, I believe that it is OK for companies and other organizations to collect people's information, as long as they do not abuse its use.

Main idea 1 Allowing businesses to gather information about their customers enables them to target their marketing to each person's interests and preferences.

Explanation/Example _____

_____

Refer to Reading 1 on pages 144 and 145 for some ideas.

Main idea 2 _____

Explanation/Example _____

_____

Look at your answers to Think and Discuss on page 147 and 148.

Main idea 3 _____

Explanation/Example _____

_____

Counter-argument Some people argue that allowing access to private information could lead to abuses, such as unlawful searches and arrest of innocent people.

Refutation _____

_____

Conclusion As long as there are legal systems in place that prevent abuses, I do not oppose the collection of people's personal information for legitimate uses.

Opinion 2   I am strongly opposed to the collection of people's information by companies and businesses. Privacy is very important to me with the priority always being protection from intrusive marketing practices, _____, and _____.

Main idea 1   When companies have information about individual consumers, they will bombard people with personalized ads.

Explanation/Example   _____

_____

Main idea 2   _____

Refer to Reading 1 on pages 144 and 145 for some ideas.

Explanation/Example   _____

_____

Main idea 3   _____

Look at your answers to Think and Discuss on page 147 and 148 and Ideas in Action on page 153.

Explanation/Example   _____

_____

Counter-argument   Despite these concerns, many people contend that some loss of privacy is necessary for governments to obtain the information needed to detect and prevent crime.

Refutation   _____

_____

Conclusion   I believe that it is best to disallow any form of privacy invasion so that citizens can be protected from the misuse of personal information.

 Analysis

Determining the Author's Purpose

Because authors have many reasons for writing different kinds of passages, recognizing the author's purpose is essential for reading comprehension. As the reader, your task is to discover these reasons so you can better understand the messages in the passage.

To understand the author's purpose, ask yourself: Why did the author write this passage? Typically, there are three main purposes for writing.

- **To inform or explain:** The author wants to educate the reader about a topic.
- **To give an opinion or to persuade:** The author wants to convince the reader to agree or disagree with a topic.
- **To entertain:** The author wants to amuse the reader with an enjoyable topic, such as one that makes people laugh or feel excited.

Choose the best answer and explain your choice.

1. What is the author's purpose for writing Reading 1?

   a. To inform or explain   b. To give an opinion or persuade   c. To entertain

   Why? _____

   _____

2. What is the purpose of the following writings?

   a. A letter to the editor of a newspaper arguing against a new law that increases taxes

      a) To inform or explain   b) To given an opinion or to persuade   c) To entertain

      Why? _____

      _____

   b. A story in a children's magazine that tells the adventures of a boy and his dog

      a) To inform or explain   b) To given an opinion or to persuade   c) To entertain

      Why? _____

      _____

   c. An article in a medical journal about treatments for cancer

      a) To inform or explain   b) To given an opinion or to persuade   c) To entertain

      Why? _____

      _____

Writing Worksheet

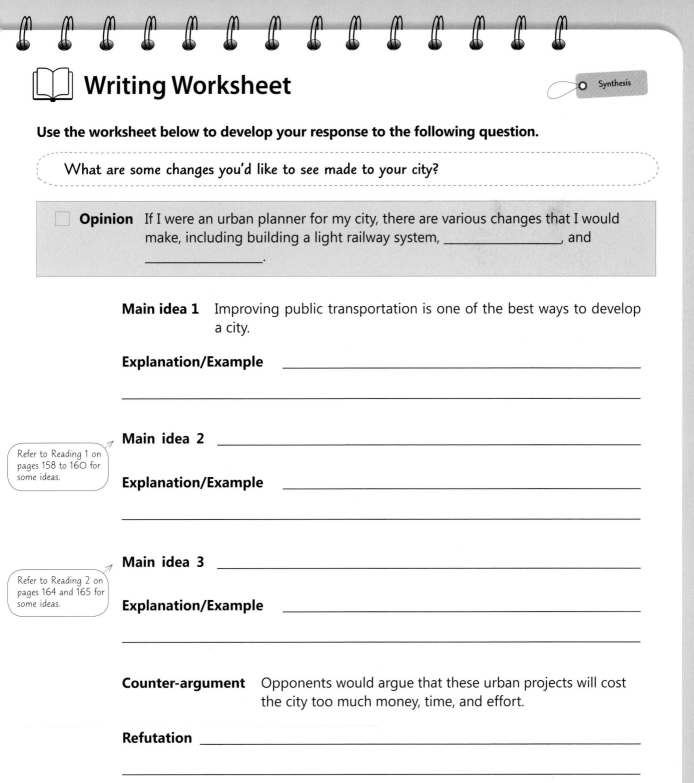

Use the worksheet below to develop your response to the following question.

> What are some changes you'd like to see made to your city?

☐ **Opinion**   If I were an urban planner for my city, there are various changes that I would make, including building a light railway system, _____, and _____.

Main idea 1   Improving public transportation is one of the best ways to develop a city.

Explanation/Example   _____

_____

Main idea 2   _____

> Refer to Reading 1 on pages 158 to 160 for some ideas.

Explanation/Example   _____

_____

Main idea 3   _____

> Refer to Reading 2 on pages 164 and 165 for some ideas.

Explanation/Example   _____

_____

Counter-argument   Opponents would argue that these urban projects will cost the city too much money, time, and effort.

Refutation _____

_____

Conclusion   With these reasons in mind, I urge city officials to seriously consider my recommendations.

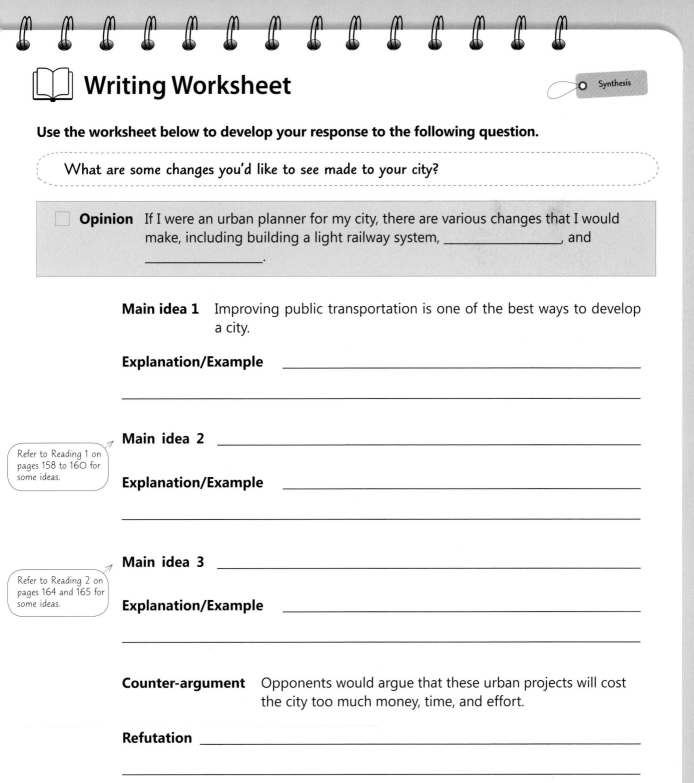

APPENDIX

Academic Word List Vocabulary

UNIT 1

READING 1

arbitrary *adj.*	based on random choice or personal whim, and not on any reason or system
consumer *n.*	a person who pays for goods and services for personal use
device *n.*	a thing made for a certain purpose, especially mechanical or electronic equipment
neutral *adj.*	not supporting either side in a conflict, disagreement, etc.; impartial
presumably *adv.*	very likely, though not known for certain
revenue *n.*	income, especially of a company or organization
shift *v.*	to change position, direction, or tendency
underestimate *v.*	to guess that something is smaller or less important than it really is

READING 2

consult *v.*	to ask for help or advice from someone
expertise *n.*	special skill or knowledge in a particular field
implicitly *adv.*	not directly expressed
motive *n.*	a reason for doing something
occupation *n.*	a job or profession
passively *adv.*	accepting or allowing what happens or what others do
undertaking *n.*	a task or project
voluntary *adj.*	done by one's own choice

UNIT 2

READING 1

assemble *v.*	to gather together in one place for a common purpose
attributable *adj.*	considered to be caused by something
commence *v.*	to begin; to start
comprehensive *adj.*	complete; including all or nearly all elements or aspects of something
contemporary *adj.*	belonging to or occurring in the present; modern
immigrant *n.*	a person who comes to live permanently in a foreign country
interpret *v.*	to explain the meaning of something
subsidize *v.*	to support financially

READING 2

administrator *n.*   a person responsible for running a business, organization, etc.

civil *adj.*   relating to citizens and their concerns

commitment *n.*   a promise to do something in the future

credit *v.*   to say that someone (or something) is responsible for something of good quality

evaluation *n.*   a judgment about the amount, number, value, or quality of something

mechanism *n.*   the process by which something happens

ongoing *adj.*   continuing; still happening

professional *adj.*   of, relating to, or connected with a certain job or career

UNIT 3

READING 1

convention *n.*   a way in which something is usually done, especially within a particular area or activity

energetic *adj.*   showing or involving great activity or vitality

eventual *adj.*   occurring at the end of or as a result of a series of events; final; ultimate

incapable *adj.*   unable to do or achieve something

institute *v.*   to start or establish something, especially a program, system, etc.

justify *v.*   to show or prove to be right or reasonable

legislate *v.*   to make laws

unmotivated *adj.*   not having interest in or enthusiasm for something, especially work or study

READING 2

adapt *v.*   to change to adjust to new conditions

corporation *n.*   a large company

domain *n.*   a sphere of influence or control

implication *n.*   a conclusion that can be drawn from something, although not explicitly stated

insightful *adj.*   showing deep understanding; perceptive

phenomenal *adj.*   amazing; remarkable; extraordinary

potentially *adv.*   possibly; having a good chance of happening

precedence *n.*   the condition of having higher importance, order, or rank; priority

UNIT 4

UNIT 5

constraint *n.*	a limit or restriction
currency *n.*	a system of money in general use in a country
depressed *adj.*	experiencing general sadness and hopelessness
evaluate *v.*	to form an idea of the amount, number, or value of; to assess
extract *v.*	to remove or take out, especially by effort or force
investment *n.*	a thing that is worth buying because it may be profitable or useful in the future
participant *n.*	a person who takes part in something
scheme *n.*	a secret or dishonest plan

UNIT 6

analogous *adj.*	similar or comparable in certain ways
context *n.*	a circumstance or situation
conversely *adv.*	in an opposite way
correspondence *n.*	a close similarity, connection, or equivalence
denote *v.*	to be a sign of; to indicate
imagery *n.*	visual images
retention *n.*	the continued keeping or use of something
so-called *adv.*	commonly referred to by a certain name or term

channel *v.*	to lead toward or guide in a certain direction
decline *v.*	to become smaller, fewer, or less; to decrease
document *v.*	to keep careful records of an event
endorse *v.*	to support or actively encourage
induce *v.*	to bring about or cause
journal *n.*	a publication that deals with a particular subject or group
enhancement *n.*	the act of improving or increasing something's value, quality, etc.
retain *v.*	to continue to have something; to keep something

UNIT 7

READING 1

data *n.*   facts and information collected and used to calculate, analyze, or plan something

invalidate *v.*   to prove that an argument, theory, or idea is wrong

range *n.*   the area between the highest and lowest values

reliance *n.*   dependence on or trust in someone or something

reversal *n.*   a change to an opposite direction, position, or course of action

statistically *adv.*   of or relating to the collection and analysis of data and information

unresolved *adj.*   not settled or decided as a solution to a problem or disagreement

variability *n.*   changeable; the quality of having a wide variety of possible values, etc.

READING 2

compute *v.*   to calculate a number or amount

deny *v.*   to say that something is untrue or does not exist

imply *v.*   to suggest the truth or existence of something without stating it clearly

infer *v.*   to form an idea about something from evidence and reasoning rather than from clear statements

initial *adj.*   existing or occurring at the beginning; starting

orient *v.*   to adjust or point something in a certain direction, etc.

persist *v.*   to continue to exist; to last

proportion *n.*   a part or share of a whole

UNIT 8

READING 1

assessment *n.*   the evaluation or estimation of the nature, quality, or ability of someone or something

assumption *n.*   something accepted as true or as certain to happen, without proof

dramatically *adv.*   in a sudden and striking way; exciting or impressive

insufficiently *adv.*   in a way that is not enough; inadequately

projected *adj.*   estimated or forecasted based on the current situation or trends

rationalize *v.*   to try to explain or justify actions, attitudes, or beliefs with reasons

recovery *n.*   a return to a normal state of health, mind, or strength

unfounded *adj.*   having no foundation or basis in fact

dominance *n.*	power and influence over others
logical *adj.*	having the quality of clear, sound reasoning
motivation *n.*	the reason(s) one has for acting or behaving in a certain way
odds *n.*	the chances or likelihood of something happening or being the case
proceed *v.*	to move forward, especially after reaching a certain point; to continue
prospect *n.*	the possibility or likelihood of some future event occurring
simulated *adj.*	fake, but made to seem real
technical *adj.*	of or relating to mechanical processes or machines

UNIT 9

READING 1

devoted *adj.*	very loving or loyal; caring
impose *v.*	to force something unwelcome or unfamiliar to be accepted
institution *n.*	an established organization
maturity *n.*	the state, fact, or period of being fully developed or grown up
reliant *adj.*	having a need for someone or something for support
stability *n.*	the state of being not likely to change or fail; permanence
unprecedented *adj.*	never done or known before; happening for the first time
utility *n.*	a service such as a supply of electricity, water, gas, etc. that is provided to the public

READING 2

accompany *v.*	to be present or occur at the same time as something
assistance *n.*	help with a job or task
constrain *v.*	to limit the scope, extent, or activity of something
eliminate *v.*	to completely erase, remove, or destroy something
redefine *v.*	to change the meaning of something; to give a new meaning to
residence *n.*	a person's home; the place where someone lives
restore *v.*	to return someone or something to a previous condition, place, or position
transition *n.*	a change from one state or condition to another

UNIT 10

READING 1

communicative *adj.* ready to talk or give information

ethnicity *n.* the state of belonging to a social group with common national or cultural traditions

hypothesize *v.* to propose an explanation based on limited evidence, usually as the start of further inquiry

intensify *v.* to become or make stronger or more intense

psychologically *adv.* of or related to the mental and emotional state of a person

resolution *n.* a solution to a problem or disagreement

revelation *n.* a surprising and previously unknown fact

violation *n.* the act of breaking a rule, law, agreement, or understanding

READING 2

abandonment *n.* the act of leaving or taking away support

accumulated *adj.* increased or built up in quantity over time

automatically *adv.* naturally and spontaneously, without conscious thought

catastrophe *n.* an event causing great and often sudden damage or suffering; a disaster

complexity *n.* the state or quality of being complicated

parameter *n.* a limit or boundary defining the scope of a process or activity

significantly *adv.* in a way that is important and worthy of attention

traditionally *adv.* of or about the long-established or inherited way of thinking or acting

UNIT 11

READING 1

aggregate *v.* to gather together to form a whole

code *n.* a set of rules or guidelines related to behavior or activity in a particular area

commission *n.* a group of people with an official function

compile *v.* to collect and combine in order to produce something

consent *n.* permission for something to happen or agreement to do something

emerging *adj.* new; just recently becoming known

implement *v.* to put a decision, plan, agreement, etc. into effect

reluctant *adj.* hesitant and unwilling to do something

clause *n.*	a part of a treaty, bill, or contract
coherent *adj.*	logical and consistent; making sense
compound *v.*	to make something worse; to make the negative aspects of something more intense
constitution *n.*	the basic principles by which a state or other organization operates
hypothetically *adv.*	supposed but not necessarily real or true; in theory
inviolable *adj.*	(of a law or right) safe from being broken or infringed upon; guaranteed
suspend *v.*	to stop from being in force or effect, usually temporarily
terminate *v.*	to bring to an end, especially an agreement or period of employment

UNIT 12

construction *n.*	the building of something, typically a large structure
consumption *n.*	the using up of a resource
framework *n.*	a basic structure underlying a system, concept, or text
innovative *adj.*	featuring new ideas and methods; advanced and original
legislation *n.*	laws passed by a government
mode *n.*	a way in which something occurs or is experienced, expressed, or done
network *n.*	a group or system of interconnected people or things
sustainable *adj.*	able to continue at a certain rate or level

appreciation *n.*	the recognition and enjoyment of the good qualities of someone or something
coincide *v.*	to agree with something; to be the same in some ways
external *adj.*	belonging to or forming the outer surface or structure of something
infrastructure *n.*	the basic structures of a place, organization, system, etc.
misconduct *n.*	unacceptable or improper behavior
occurrence *n.*	an incident or event
offset *v.*	to make up for or balance something by having an opposing force or effect; to counteract
revolution *n.*	a very great change

On Point Website and Mobile App

If you are using *On Point*, enrich your learning experience with our website and mobile app.

Website
To use the website, go to **www.compassdigibooks.com**

Mobile app
To use the mobile app, download it from Google Play or the Apple App Store and install it on your Android or iOS mobile device.

App Store   **Google** play

How to register
1. If you are a new user, click "Student Register" or "Teacher Register."
2. Read and agree to the Terms and Conditions, and click "Next."
3. Create a username and password or register with your Facebook or Google+ account.
4. Click "Please add a book for online practice." Then, enter the access code below, and click on "Complete."
5. Click on the cover of the book.

What you can do

For Teachers   Click on…

Manage Classes	**Online Practice**	**Download Resources**
to set up classes for your students, view their progress, email students, collect homework, and get class reports	to preview the vocabulary, reading, listening, and writing activities your students are doing	to download the Teacher's Guide, classroom slide presentations, unit tests, Answer Key, and mp3 audio files

For Students   Click on…

Online Practice	**Listening Audio**	**Join a Class**
to get more practice with vocabulary, reading, listening, and writing activities for each unit	to listen to audio recordings of all of the passages in the book	to join a class using the code from your teacher

Your access code